D.R THORPE.

D0101727

Mount Everest National Park

Sagarmatha
Mother of the Universe

Margaret Jefferies

The Mountaineers
in association with
David Bateman

First published in the United States 1991 by
The Mountaineers
306 Second Avenue West
Seattle WA 98119 USA

The Mountaineers: Organized 1906 ". . . to explore, study,
preserve and enjoy the natural beauty . . ."

Address all trade enquiries to The Mountaineers (except India
and Nepal to India Book Distributors, 107/108, Arcadia, 195,
Nariman Point, Bombay; Australia and New Zealand to David
Bateman Ltd , Auckland, New Zealand).

ISBN 0-89886-267-1

Published in association with
David Bateman Ltd
"Golden Heights", 32-34 View Road
Glenfield, Auckland, New Zealand

Printed and bound in Hong Kong

KING MAHENDRA TRUST FOR NATURE CONSERVATION

MESSAGE FROM THE CHAIRMAN

I am delighted to witness a Handbook on the Sagarmatha National Park published with the collective efforts of both Nepalese and New Zealanders. For me, it is a development personally gratifying, as I had the honour to announce to the world the decision of His Majesty's Government of Nepal, the establishment of a national park in the world's highest region at the Third International Congress of the World Wildlife Fund in Bonn in October 1973. The significance of the Sagarmatha National Park has been enhanced by the fact that UNESCO has thought fit to include it in the World Heritage List.

While thanking the government of New Zealand for their constructive cooperation in the development of this area, I cannot be a silent observer to the reality that the pressure put on the area in the form of unwarranted and unguided tourism, has had its share of negative impact on the region's environment necessitating corrective measures before it is too late.

Realising this the King Mahendra Trust for Nature Conservation has considered to sponsor a project to 'save' Sagarmatha on a priority basis. The handbook, besides providing insights into the natural and human history of the region will, I hope, help highlight the need to protect it from the effects of human encroachment, thus contributing towards enlisting international support to save Sagarmatha.

HIS ROYAL HIGHNESS PRINCE GYANENDRA BIR BIKRAM SHAH

NATIONAL PARKS BUILDING, BABAR MAHAL, P.O. BOX 3712, KATHMANDU, NEPAL
TELEX: NP 2203 ● CABLE: NATRUST ● TEL 215850, 215912

Symbols of Buddhism and towering mountains — the essence of Khumbu and its people. The 'all seeing' eyes of a chorten gaze in four directions to surrounding peaks, while prayer flags blow in the wind, sending messages skyward to the gods.

"Om mani padme hum" — Hail to the Jewel of the Lotus. The repetitive Buddhist chant is carved onto stone tablets which here form a wall dividing the trail. Many stone walls are found all over the Khumbu and are a mark of devotion, with religious merit gained by those who pass on the left, and also by the person who had the stones carved. As a mark of respect visitors should also pass to the left of these walls and stones.

Pride of the Himalaya and national flower of Nepal, *Rhododendron arboreum* displays its brillance. This beautiful species occurs from 1600 to nearly 4000 metres, growing to eighteen metres in height and often forming large forests. In the spring whole mountainsides are stained red with their vivid and glorious abundance.

Foreword

'We were at the right place at the right time.' These words best describe how Tenzing and I happened to be standing on top of Mount Everest on May 29th, 1953.

I had first visited the Khumbu region nearly two years before as a member of Eric Shipton's British Reconnaissance Expedition and I remember very clearly the beautiful path winding through dense forests and shrublands which framed the mighty peaks above. The mountains are still there and so is the path, attracting dozens of expeditions and thousands of trekkers from every nation, but over the last thirty years I have seen those forests and parklands being dramatically destroyed in response to the urgent needs of the visitors for firewood for heating and cooking. In the past the Sherpa people of the Everest (Sagarmatha) region had been very careful in protecting their forests but now there is increasing financial pressure to persuade them to cut, and cut, and cut!

I suppose, in some way, I was initially responsible for the increasing damage to the forests. In my efforts to help the Sherpa people by constructing hospitals, schools, bridges and water supplies, my team built the airstrip at Lukla to assist in the transport of materials. Its construction had the unexpected effect of giving much easier access to the area, and an increasing number of tourists accelerated the demand for firewood.

The visitors who came — trekkers, mountaineers and others who were interested in the special qualities of the Sherpas — placed great demands on the environment and caused changes to the lifestyle and culture of the local people, and the forest resources shrunk noticeably. Most of us who were deeply concerned about the area felt that the only way to protect it was by the establishment of a National Park.

With assistance from the New Zealand Government, a National Park became a reality and the area has started on its long and shaky road to recovery. A great deal of work and goodwill is still needed to regenerate the forests and protect the qualities that make this such a special part of the world.

This book has been compiled to give visitors an introduction to the people and nature of Sagarmatha National Park. It not only describes how to get from point 'A' to point 'B' but tries to give a background of the history, culture and ecology of the area. It is hoped that the reader will become aware of the delicate balances that nature and a strong Buddhist faith have established, and how these balances can be retained by sensitive visitors who accept an attitude of responsibility to this beautiful land and its resident Sherpas.

Sir Edmund Hillary

Detail of a traditional style painting of the Khumbu region, as seen through the eyes of an artist.

Contents

Faces of Khumbu reflect the changing world of
a hardy mountain people. The old once knew an
existence which had changed little over the
centuries, while todays youngsters adapt to a
lifestyle which is affected by western influences.

Khumbu

A Land Rediscovered

The country wild and mountainous and is little frequented by strangers whose visit the King discourages — Marco Polo.

For centuries Nepal was closed to the outside world, and little was known of the mountainous kingdom sandwiched between India and Tibet. It is also a land of great contrasts. Both the landscape and its people share this quality, for in this beautiful kingdom two civilisations merge: the Indic and Sinic; two religions, Hinduism and Buddhism; two races, Caucasian and Mongoloid. To the south are ethnic groups of Indian origin while to the north are those of Tibetan origin, who in Nepal are called the Bhotia, the word *bhot* meaning Tibet. Of the Bhotia people, it is the Sherpas who are the most widely known beyond Nepal's borders, for both their mountaineering ability and outstanding qualities of character.

Beneath the southern slopes of Sagarmatha (Mt Everest) lies the land of the Sherpas, although smaller communities stretch from north of Kathmandu east-ward to Darjeeling in India. The very heart of Sherpa country is centred around three areas in the upper reaches and tributaries of the Dudh Kosi or Milk River. At the headwaters is the high, fan-shaped area known as Khumbu, which channels into the gorges of Pharak and then opens to the fertile slopes and valleys of the Solu; combined they are known as the Solu-Khumbu district.

It is believed that four to five hundred years ago the Khumbu region was discovered and settled by Tibetan migrants. After the harsh climate of Tibet they did not find the climate of Khumbu too dissimilar or difficult to live in. The area was probably not already inhabited by other ethnic groups because people from the warm Indian sub-continent had no liking for the cold inhospitable mountains and had no desire to live there.

Being traders by nature and origin, and secondly subsistence farmers, the hardy newcomers soon established themselves in places where their traditional crops could be grown and their animals grazed. The pass over which they had crossed to enter Nepal made a natural trade route and their yaks were soon bringing rock salt, wool and skins from Tibet in exchange for grains, cottons, cattle crossbreeds and possibly butter from Nepal and India.

The life of a trader was hard, but for middle men in the trade and exchange of material goods it had its rewards and the Sherpas, as these Tibetans became known, were able to maintain their existence. The isolation of this mountain kingdom was continued until the middle of the twentieth century, with the lives of its people proceeding in the same ways, as they had for generations.

By 1950 the doors were opened to visitors from the outside.world. The first mountaineering expeditions came seeking the summits of the Himalaya and the grand prize of Sagarmatha, paving the way for the modern trekker. Khumbu was rediscovered.

Rugged and remote, the mountains and valleys of Khumbu are home to the hardy Sherpas.

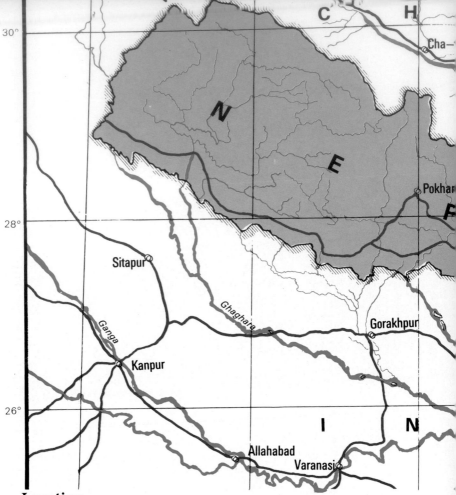

Location

Sagarmatha National Park covers the area known as Khumbu and is situated in the north-eastern region of Nepal. It is spectacular, mountainous country of approximately 1200 square kilometres, all above 3000 metres in altitude. The area contains the upper catchments of the Dudh Kosi, Imja Khola and Bhote Kosi Rivers. These rivers drain the southern slopes of some of the world's highest mountains, the most significant being Sagarmatha, and form one of the headwaters of the Ganges River.

The area is bordered in the north by Chinese Tibet and is surrounded by high mountainous ridges, nowhere lower than 5700 metres. Access from the south via the Dudh Kosi is also restricted by deep narrow gorges. These natural barriers kept Khumbu untouched by outside influences until the advent of modern tourism and transportation.

Most of the Park is steep and rugged, the terrain broken by deep gorges and glacial valleys, but in its major valleys there are some relatively level areas which are used for cropping and grazing by approximately 3500

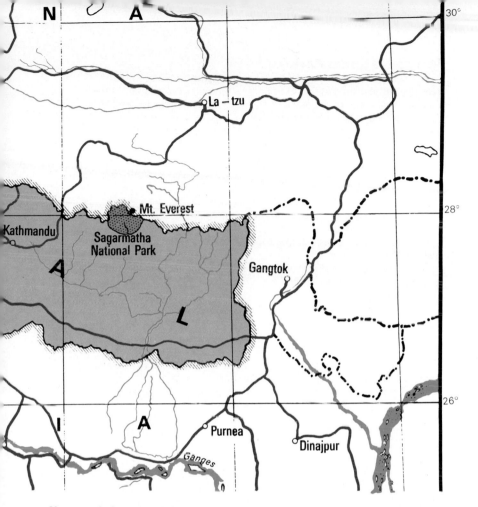

Sherpa inhabitants. Their village areas are officially excluded from the Park and do not come under its authority.

Other residents of Khumbu include Tibetans, remnants of the 4000 refugees who passed through after the Chinese occupation of Tibet in the late 1950's, as well as those who had earlier come over the Nangpa La to work for the Sherpas, and many from other Nepalese ethnic groups. The latter are mainly Government officials and military employees, labourers, tradesmen and servants from the lower regions of Nepal, where economic hardship has forced them to seek permanent residence and employment in Sherpa households.

To the Hindu ethnic groups, the Sherpas' position in the caste system was in the rank above the untouchables; however, as Buddhists the Sherpas see themselves in a different role. Both Hindu and Buddhist respect each other's faith, and in the words of His Majesty King Birendra: *Mutual tolerance and peaceful co-existence have been the basis of social harmony and cultural synthesis since the dawn of our country's history.*

Why a National Park?

Apart from the obvious reason that the Khumbu Region contains the world's highest mountain, the fact that its rivers form some of the headwaters of one of the world's greatest rivers is of significant importance. The condition of this catchment has the potential to influence the lives of people living beyond the boundaries of the Park, and even beyond the boundaries of Nepal.

Geologically the area is of very recent origin, so it is of great scientific interest because it contains fine examples of the flora and fauna of this part of the Himalaya. The entire catchment of the Dudh Kosi is contained within the Park, on the southern side of the Himalaya; whereas major rivers to the east and west, the Arun and Tamba Kosi, have their catchments in the Tibetan Plateau to the north of the main mountain chain. These river systems had taken shape before the period of major uplift of the Himalaya, but the Dudh Kosi was formed later. Because of its recent origins and relative isolation from Tibet and the rest of Nepal, the plant, animal, insect and bird species found in the Dudh Kosi catchment have developed more independently from those of other areas.

Khumbu is also of major religious and cultural significance in Nepal. The Sherpas' lifestyle is unique compared to other high altitude dwellers and they follow a very old form of Tibetan Buddhism. To many visitors it may seem contrary to conservation ethics that Sagarmatha National Park has a resident population of people who still live their traditional lifestyle, farming crops and animals within the park boundaries. It is now recognised, however, that with increasing world populations and dwindling land resources it is no longer possible or desirable to set aside areas of land which are 'untouched by man'. The Sherpas have lived in relative harmony with the land for nearly five centuries and are very much part of the natural history of the Park with their unique culture and lifestyle.

Although wild mammal numbers and species are low in Khumbu, the area is the habitat of the endangered Musk Deer, which has been given special protective status by legislation. The rare Snow Leopard is also thought to exist in the high areas of the Park, in spite of a lack of recent sightings, for there are many remote corners.

With all these factors considered, apart from the tremendous scenic beauty, the area certainly filled the criteria for National Park status, to protect it for all to enjoy in the future.

A rich cultural heritage and outstanding scenery are important features of the Khumbu region. The gompa at Pangboche, oldest in the area, is built on a site where according to legend the Sherpas' patron saint, Lama Sangwa Dorje, made an imprint of his hand on a rock as he flew from Tibet.

Formation

With the political upheavals in Tibet in 1959 there was an influx of Tibetan refugees pouring over the borders into Nepal. Many of these brought their grazing animals with them and settled in Khumbu. This increase in resident peoples and grazing animals, along with increasing pressure from growing numbers of tourists requiring food and warmth, had obvious detrimental effects on the fragile high-altitude forests and grasslands.

There were many proposals to form the Khumbu into a National Park and these were subject to a number of studies commissioned by His Majesty's Government. Reports by the Food and Agricultural Organisation (F.A.O.), United Nations and other conservationists all strongly endorsed the formation of a national park. The decision in principle to establish it was made by His Royal Highness Prince Gyanendra of Nepal at the World Congress of the World Wildlife Fund, at Bonn in October 1973.

"We sincerely believe that this region and its surroundings in the grandeur of the Khumbu Valley are of major significance not only to us but the whole world as an ecological, cultural and geographical treasure which, we hope, should provide peace and tranquillity and be a significant contribution to a better World Heritage."
— His Royal Highness Prince Gyanendra Bir Bikram Shah, Bonn, 5th October 1973.

Because of New Zealand's experience with mountain park management, and other factors, His Majesty's Government of Nepal approached the New Zealand Government to help establish this new National Park, and in 1974 an appraisal of the proposed area was made by officials from New Zealand. Through a bi-lateral Nepal/New Zealand Aid agreement, a project to establish the Park was commenced in 1975, and for the next six years the New Zealand Government maintained advisers in the area, providing basic amenities and guidelines. As part of this project Sherpas were trained in New Zealand in national park and reserves management, and they have since returned to Nepal to help manage its protected areas. The Park is now managed entirely by the Department of National Parks and Wildlife Conservation, of His Majesty's Government.

Sagarmatha National Park was officially gazetted by His Majesty's Government of Nepal on 19th July 1976, and was the third area in Nepal to be set aside as a National Park. In 1979 Sagarmatha was declared a World Heritage Site in recognition of the cultural importance of the Sherpa people, the significance of the world's highest mountain, and its associated flora and fauna. As such it is eligible for finance from the World Heritage Fund, administered by UNESCO.

Like a watchful matriarch, Sagarmatha towers regally above the neighbouring wall of Nuptse and Lhotse, to survey deep gorges of the Dudh Kosi valley below.

Rock, Ice and Snow
Sagarmatha — "Mother of the Universe"

Sagarmatha 'Mother of the Universe' is truly the bringer of life to the millions who live in the shadow of her presence. From her high ramparts and the other lesser peaks of the Himalaya come tributaries of the mighty Ganges river, a resource without which those millions could not exist. Fed by snow falling during the summer months, huge glacier neves are annually added to, while at the glacier terminals the old ice, rubble and silt-laden, thaws rapidly in the moist warm air. Swollen and milky, the rivers rush out from the glaciers, carrying with them tonnes of silt, and gathering more as they surge down the gorges which split the mountain chains.

Some of this material is deposited on the flat plains of the Ganges basin, renewing the land once more. As the gigantic brown Ganges swirls onwards down to the Bay of Bengal, resistance is met from the waters of the ocean and the remaining silt is dropped. Eventually this sediment will become compacted, perhaps to be forced above the sea to form new land in some future time. Each year the cycle is repeated; the mountains are eroded, and the land is returned to the sea from which it originally came.

A journey to the sea begins. Carrying fine particles of rock, ground from the highest summits by glacial ice, meltwaters of the Khumbu Glacier flow down to the Ganges River, to eventually reach the ocean. During this journey the silt is deposited to build more land, in an endless cycle of destruction and renewal.

(opposite): Mantled in snow and ice, Nuptse guards the black ramparts of Sagarmatha. Both mountains contribute to the surrounding glaciers by feeding them with avalanche snow from their upper slopes. In time this will compact to ice, and as the glaciers descend to the lower levels, melts to form the rivers.

23

Beginnings

The rocks which make up the highest summits of the Himalaya came originally from beneath the sea, deposited as sediments between three hundred to seven hundred million years ago. These layers of mud, sand and lime-rich sediment were buried by more and more sediment, which increased the pressure and temperature so that the rocks were altered in structure (metamorphosed). Later, large intrusions of molten material, usually in the form of granites, also altered the thick sedimentary sequence and the mudstone, sandstone and limestone changed to slates, schists, marbles and gneisses. These have subsequently been upthrust and can be seen in the high Himalaya with good examples in the great bands across the Lhotse-Nuptse Wall.

Deposited millions of years ago beneath the sea, layer upon layer of sedimentary rock forms the great wall of Nuptse and Lhotse which catches the last colour of the setting sun. Two great continents on the move have since upthrust these rocks over 8000 metres to form the highest summits of the Himalaya.

The Continents Collide

The Himalaya were formed as a result of the collision between India and Eurasia, two of the large continental plates that make up the earth's crust. Originally the collision of these plates was regarded as a simple, isolated and recent event, but geological evidence now indicates that such collisions have occurred in the area for the last 120 million years or more. This has resulted in the accretion of several slithers of continental crustal material onto a part of the Eurasian plate which now forms Tibet.

The most recent collision began about sixty million years ago when the Indian plate was located in the southern hemisphere and was already drifting northwards at about eleven centimetres a year. About fifty million years ago, the Indian plate collided with Eurasia. This produced volcanism in northern Tibet and thrust southern Tibet over the leading edge of the Indian plate. The collision also juxtaposed rocks in Tibet and Nepal that were originally deposited thousands of kilometres apart.

The northward drift of the Indian plate slowed against the resistance of the Eurasian plate, but it is still drifting today, at about five centimetres every year, and in the past sixty million years it appears that about 1000 kilometres of the Indian plate has been pushed under the Eurasian plate. With time, the location of this overlapping of the plates has progressively moved south, causing slithers of Indian crustal material to be added onto the part of the Eurasian plate that is now being upthrust.

The high Himalaya are one of these slithers. The present site of major upthrusting is on the Main Boundary Thrust (MBT), a major fault in Southern Nepal and northern India.

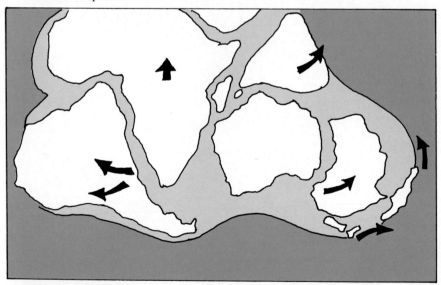

The earth's crust is composed of major rigid virtually undistorted slabs or plates. These plates have been moving for hundreds of millions of years and are still moving.

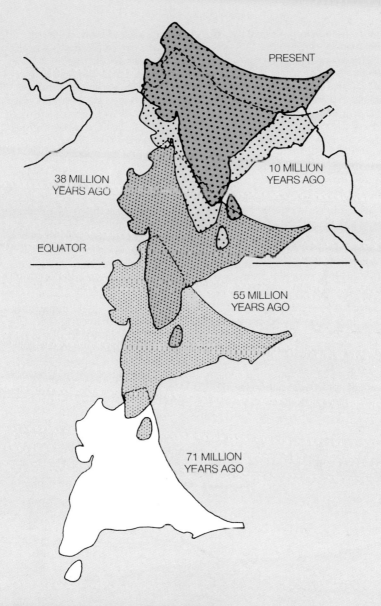

PRESENT

38 MILLION
YEARS AGO

10 MILLION
YEARS AGO

EQUATOR

55 MILLION
YEARS AGO

71 MILLION
YEARS AGO

Convection currents deep within the earth bring two land masses together. Originally located in the southern hemisphere, the Indian plate has slowly drifted northward and inevitably collided with Eurasia. The Eurasian plate has been thrust over the Indian plate, and subsequent shattering and buckling of the edges of these land masses, as they continue to be forced together, has pushed the Himalaya upwards.

"Continents in Collision" Keith Miller, 1982
Royal Geographical Society, London.

With the collision of these two plates, a large area of land, from the Himalayan foothills to the Tibetan Plateau, has been uplifted. This uplift, however, is occurring at varying rates in different areas. It appears that the Himalaya is rising about 0.2mm a year faster than Tibet. This difference in uplift implies that the Himalaya was lower than Tibet some two million years ago, spectacular evidence for this being provided by the many rivers which originate north of the Himalaya and flow southward across the main ridges of the mountains. These rivers probably established their original courses on a slope which fell from a northern highland to the southern Ganges Plain. Since then the Himalayan mountains have risen higher across this slope, and faster than Tibet. As the mountains became steeper the rivers flowing down their slopes moved faster, becoming more erosive, gouging out the incredible gorges visible today.

More evidence is provided by the studies of paleoclimate on the northern flank of the Himalaya, which show that up until the middle Pleistocene (about one million years ago) the Himalaya did not significantly block the moisture-laden air from the south as they do today. Since the late Pleistocene, however, the mountain range has become a barrier, causing a dramatic change to a dry, cold, continental climate over its northern flanks and Tibet.

As well as being the highest mountains in the world, the Himalaya are among the youngest. The present rate of uplift is difficult to gauge because precise measurements go back for only a century, but there is no doubt that the highest Himalaya are growing still higher under the pressure of the merging continents. Calculations from geodetic surveys in northern India and geological information throughout Nepal and India give the annual growth at about one millimetre. This does not allow for erosion which is less than the uplift.

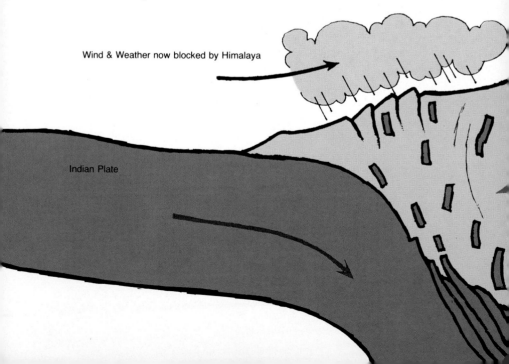

Wind & Weather now blocked by Himalaya

Indian Plate

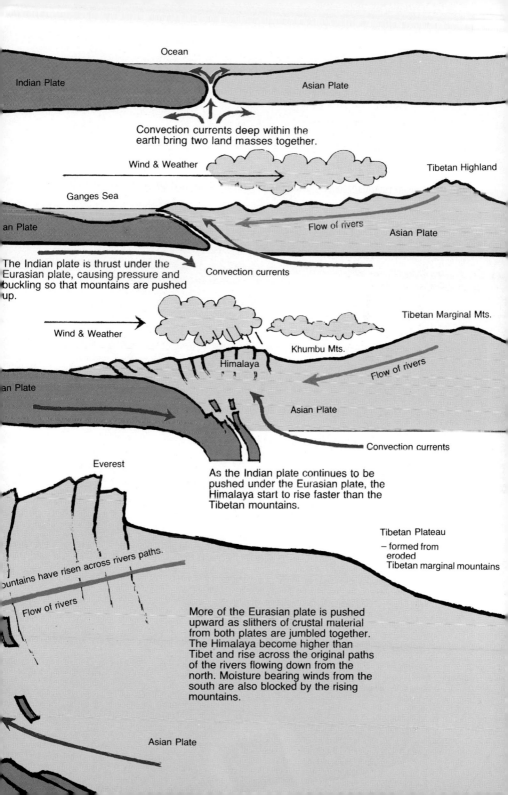

Ocean

Indian Plate

Asian Plate

Convection currents deep within the
earth bring two land masses together.

Wind & Weather

Tibetan Highland

Ganges Sea

an Plate

Flow of rivers

Asian Plate

The Indian plate is thrust under the
Eurasian plate, causing pressure and
buckling so that mountains are pushed
up.

Convection currents

Wind & Weather

Tibetan Marginal Mts.

Khumbu Mts.

Himalaya

an Plate

Flow of rivers

Asian Plate

Convection currents

Everest

As the Indian plate continues to be
pushed under the Eurasian plate, the
Himalaya start to rise faster than the
Tibetan mountains.

Tibetan Plateau

– formed from
eroded
Tibetan marginal mountains

untains have risen across rivers paths.

Flow of rivers

More of the Eurasian plate is pushed
upward as slithers of crustal material
from both plates are jumbled together.
The Himalaya become higher than
Tibet and rise across the original paths
of the rivers flowing down from the
north. Moisture bearing winds from the
south are also blocked by the rising
mountains.

Asian Plate

Landshaping glaciers grind their way down the flanks of mountains they are born on, carrying rocks carved out by their ice as they move. Here the small tributary Lobuche Glacier descends from Lobuche peak toward the much larger Khumbu Glacier at its base.

Shaping the Land

Like all steep high mountains the rocks which make up the Himalaya are continually being eroded away. Appalling disasters can accompany these natural forces of erosion and gravity, rendering futile any human attempts to control them. Everywhere one can see evidence of erosion, with some spectacular examples occurring in the Park. Just below the junction of the Imja and Lobuje Kholas, for example, the Imja has undercut a large moraine below Mt Ama Dablam, forming a scar of fresh grey material.

Glacial lake outburst floods are another phenomenon of high mountains. Avalanches of ice or rock into the lakes, or excessive melting of ice, can cause glacial lakes to overtop their unstable containing walls, which then breach rapidly, allowing a devastating outflow of water. In 1977 a glacier below Mt Ama Dablam released water into the Imja Khola. In August an even bigger flood occurred after the lake on the Langmoche Glacier, in the Bhote Kosi Valley, burst out. Both these floods swept away bridges, severely eroded river banks and caused loss of life and property for many kilometres downstream. Similar floods have occurred in the past and will surely occur again in future times.

Created overnight by forces of nature, this lake in the Imja Valley was formed in 1977 when the snout of a glacier under Mt. Ama Dablam collapsed. Debris, carried by a torrent of released water blocked the main river below, forming the lake which will eventually disappear as it fills with silt and rock flour continually carried down by the glacial river waters.

Much of the erosion occurs unnoticed during the monsoon rains, or as rocks become detached following the many freeze-thaw cycles, but the most visible contributors are the glaciers and snowfields. Since the onset of the First Ice Age nearly two million years ago, ice has been incessantly reshaping the Himalaya. The snow clings precariously to the high mountain summits, forming thin sheets of ice which accumulate and compress to form glaciers whose forces chisel the peaks to fine points. Without the glaciers the lofty summits would only be large unsculptured masses of rock, and the mountains of the Park less attractive than they are.

Sculptured by the chiselling action of glaciers, Kangtaiga's ice-capped summit rises sharply above sheer rock walls.

SOUTH

moderate rain

Heavy rain

Middle hills

Mahabharat Range

● Kathmandu

Siwalik hills

Cradled by rocky arms, a hanging glacier carves out a cirque beneath the fluted summit of Tamserku. Action by similar glaciers on the other sides of the mountains has produced its pointed shape over a long period of time.

34

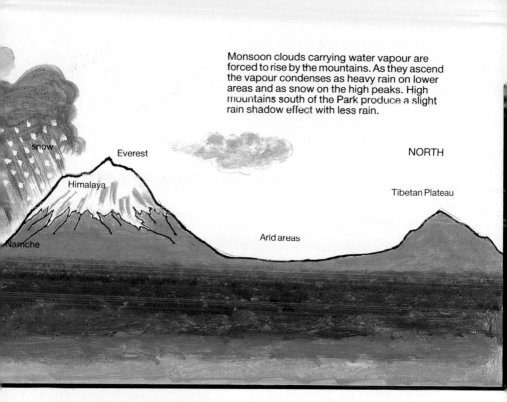

Monsoon clouds carrying water vapour are forced to rise by the mountains. As they ascend the vapour condenses as heavy rain on lower areas and as snow on the high peaks. High mountains south of the Park produce a slight rain shadow effect with less rain.

snow

Everest

NORTH

Himalaya

Tibetan Plateau

Arid areas

Namche

The glaciers are born of the monsoon. Forced to rise by the great wall of mountains, the moisture condenses, to fall as rain at lower altitudes and as snow on the mountain tops. At high altitudes the fallen snow hardly melts, and fresh layers are slowly buried and compacted by succeeding falls. The star-shaped crystals are compressed into round granules of ice as the snow accumulates, and as successive layers build up to a depth of several hundred metres, the pressure of their weight causes the lower levels to flow slowly down the mountain, dragging with them the brittle surface layers. Slowed by friction with the valley walls, the layers do not move uniformly, and the edges of the glacier continually split into crevasses. These close up again when the stresses diminish. As the glacier travels, it bites into the rock over which it moves, plucking debris from the floor and walls. At its head it scoops out an armchair-shaped cirque, and on many high peaks a ring of cirques progressively sharpens the mountain's outline. A main-trunk glacier may be joined by tributaries as it moves down a valley. As it usually gouges out its own valley deeper, and at a faster rate, the tributaries are left hanging, or linked by steep ice falls.

Most of the rock debris is carried within the glacier, but some of it accumulates on the surface in bands along the edges. These bands are called lateral moraines and when glaciers converge the moraines meet in the centre of the trunk glacier, striping it like a coloured ribbon. At the glaciers' end the melting ice exposes jumbles of rock debris, forming terminal moraines. It is here that mosses and grasses may eventually establish a tentative foothold.

35

1

1. Confluence of two frozen rivers. Pushed up by the pressure of converging ice flows, moraines of two glaciers meet in jumbled confusion.

2. Rocks and vegetation tell a story and a recent ice advance of the Khumbu Glacier is revealed by piles of light coloured moraine. They overly the old terminal moraine which is darkened by weathering, and plants which have gained a foothold.

3. Seasonal layers of winter and monsoon snow are marked by wind-blown dust. As they accumulate and compact the layers are exposed when sections of the glacier subside, or are lifted by undulations in the bedrock beneath.

4. Stresses caused by friction from the valley walls, and underlying rock bulges, wrack the ice and split it into crevasses. As the ice moves on and stresses diminish the crevasses close up and disappear.

3

2

4

5

5. Unmarked at first, except for wind ripples, snow accumulated on gentle slopes soon splits into crevasses as it moves downwards over steepening slopes, pushed along by the pressure of its weight.

1

As they move slowly down the valleys, to some 1300 metres below the snowline, the glaciers broaden their profiles from a narrow V carved by prehistoric rivers, to a smooth-based U. The main valleys in the Park are all good examples of this. Of the many glaciers in the Khumbu region the Ngozumpa is the longest in the Park. Stretching from the basin formed by the mighty summits of Cho Oyo and Gyachung Kang, it fills the Dudh Kosi Valley for twenty kilometres. Second to it is the sixteen kilometres long Nangpa Glacier, whose lateral moraines form the trading highway to the Nangpa La and Tibet. Small in comparison, but by far the best known is the Khumbu Glacier, the goal of the sight-seeing trekker, and a road for the mountaineers who battle the elements to gain the coveted crests of Sagarmatha, Lhotse and Nuptse.

The Khumbu Glacier is a typical glacier of Sagarmatha National Park. Thousands of years ago it extended at least as far as Tengboche and probably Namche Bazar. Since then, deposits from these old advances have been largely removed by erosion, or covered by younger moraines of the glaciers draining from Ama Dablam, Tamserku, Kangtaiga, and Tawoche.

1. Arising on the upper slopes of Sagarmatha and Lhotse, the Khumbu Glacier tumbles in a chaotic icefall before turning at the base of Nuptse (on right).

2. Broad and rubble covered it then flows straight for several kilometres, its moon-like surface rumpled and pitted with meltwater pools and sinkholes. 3. In contrast, lateral moraines along the sides allow climbers and trekkers an easy access to the upper reaches.

39

GLACIER FEATURES

① Accumulation area

② Bergschrund boundary between moving glacier and ice adhering to rock

③ Ice avalanche

④ Icefall, confusion of seracs, ice blocks and crevasses

⑤ Tension crevasses

⑥ Shelves and aprons of hanging ice

⑦ Landslide, rock avalanche

⑧ Lateral moraines

⑨ Englacial debris

⑩ Terminal (end) moraine

⑪ Surface debris (till or moraine)

⑫ Ice pinnacles

⑬ Surface stream

⑭ Moulin

⑮ Englacial stream

⑯ Stream portal

⑰ Region of erosion mainly by abrasion

⑱ Erosion by plucking

⑲ Sink holes

⑳ Tills of many kinds forming a terminal moraine

㉑ Ice covered moraine containing stagnant ice

Artist conception of an Himalayan
glacier

At Pheriche there are signs of more recent advances, with distinct lateral moraines found down both sides of the valley, but more noticeably on the north-eastern side. When one looks back, after leaving Pheriche and before starting the climb to Dughla, these moraines are very apparent. The rushing mountain torrent which one crosses just before Dughla originates directly from the melting ice of the Khumbu Glacier, hence its milky appearance. It carries fine particles of 'rock flour' ground by the glacier.

At the top of the climb, beyond Dughla, is the imposing slope of rock debris, partially covered by vegetation, which marks the terminal moraine of the Khumbu Glacier.

Alongside the lateral moraine on the trail to Lobuche, light-coloured rocks form gullies which breach the moraine wall. These date from a small ice advance which took place between 1600 and 1850 A.D., when ice briefly overtopped the older moraines. As the climate warmed again the ice began to melt more rapidly and a large volume of melt-water was contained within by the moraine walls. Eventually, at points of weakness, the water escaped, eroding these gullies and flushing out large volumes of sand and silt.

From the crest of the lateral moraine wall at Lobuche there is a panorama of a lunar-like landscape. The dirt and dust-stained ice, sink holes of icy

Drab and unattractive, moraine rubble performs a useful function in protecting glacial ice from the heat of the sun. Without it the glaciers would be much shorter, their ice melted by sunlight which is unfiltered by the thin air of high altitudes, and therefore more intense.

Evidence of a colder past. Thousands of years ago, when temperatures were much colder than at present, the Khumbu Glacier extended further than its present terminus. Lateral moraines from these early advances remain as terraces above the valley floor at Pheriche.

blue melt-water, and many hectares of loose moraine rubble are not the vast expanse of sparkling white that many visitors imagine they will see. Although not particularly appealing to the eye, moraine cover does help the glacier to attain a greater length by protecting the under-lying ice from the penetrating rays of the sun. At this altitude the sun, unfiltered by the thin clear air, would have otherwise melted the ice long before it had reached its present terminus.

For those trekking to the Everest Base Camp, the trail joins the Khumbu Glacier just beyond Gorak Shep and at this point the glacier ice is estimated to be about 450 metres thick. Further up the glacier the first glimpse of truly white ice comes in the form of some beautifully sculptured ice seracs, which march in two columns down its centre. Within these monoliths, which are thrown up by internal pressures caused by converging flows of ice, clearly defined and stratified layers of clean and dirty ice can be seen. They mark the annual snowfalls which have fallen and compacted within the accumulation zone of the glacier, and have survived many years while moving slowly down the valley. Each dark band represents the dry winter season when almost no snow falls. Dust blown in the dry air leaves a film over the snow's surface, marking the end of one snowfall season and the beginning of another.

At Base Camp is the spectacular scene of the Khumbu Icefall, descending in a chaotic jumble between the massifs of Sagarmatha and Nuptse. Here the glacier, hurried along by the steepening slopes and tremendous pressure, moves rapidly from its birthplace at higher altitudes into a confusion of seracs, ice blocks and crevasses. It is this icefall which presents the first major obstacle to mountaineers wishing to penetrate the upper sanctuaries and gain access to the South Col and surrounding summits. The upper limit of the Khumbu Glacier is around 6000 metres on the south-west face of Sagarmatha, and up to 8000 metres on the Lhotse face.

It is in this area that glaciologists have discovered a peculiarity of the Sagarmatha National Park glaciers. Using precipitation records, and relating them to the area of the glacier's catchment, they have found that direct snowfall could only supply about a quarter of its volume. It is far too small to account for the mass of ice that the Khumbu Glacier holds, and it is thought that the balance is contributed by avalanche and windblown snow from the surrounding peaks. This helps to explain the very bare rocky appearance of the mountains surrounding the Khumbu Glacier.

Like a bomb-shattered city, with rubble-blocked streets and toppling buildings, the Khumbu Glacier presents a dangerous highway to the upper sanctuary of the Western Cwm. From the Base Camp site climbers threading a delicate route through its chaos are lost from sight in the maze of crevasses and blocks.

Thrust upward by pressures within, an ice pinnacle erupts from the glacier surface. Shelves and aprons of ice hanging above the main glacier contribute to its mass as blocks break away and avalanche to the valley floor.

Weather Patterns

Torn away by the jet stream winds, snow particles plume from the summit of Lhotse.

Jet Streams

Although weather may seem to be just a local phenomenon, it is in reality part of a highly complex global system involving many variables such as temperature, air pressure, wind, humidity and precipitation. The bonds which join these are the jet streams — large high speed air currents which circle the earth in ever changing patterns, at altitudes of between seven and forty kilometres. Jet streams in the innermost layer of the atmosphere, up to an altitude of fifteen kilometres, travel at speeds of between sixty and ninety kilometres per hour. They move blizzards, rain-storms and squall lines, and drag lower-lying air packages across the land, thereby affecting local weather conditions.

Despite the great altitudes at which they circulate, jet streams are themselves affected by terrestial features. High land masses such as the Tibetan Plateau and Himalaya cause them to meander. The Tibetan Plateau is sheltered behind the 2,500 kilometres long Himalayan chain and because these mountains do not lie at right angles to the airflow, the jet stream can circle around them.

Contrasting air pressures over Tibet and India cause changes to the direction of jet streams during summer and winter.

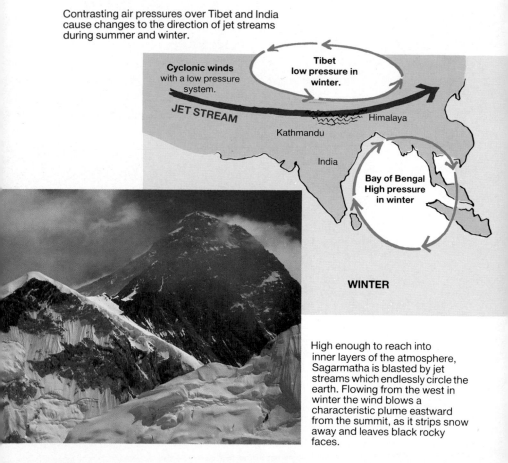

Cyclonic winds with a low pressure system.

JET STREAM

Tibet low pressure in winter.

Himalaya

Kathmandu

India

Bay of Bengal High pressure in winter

WINTER

High enough to reach into inner layers of the atmosphere, Sagarmatha is blasted by jet streams which endlessly circle the earth. Flowing from the west in winter the wind blows a characteristic plume eastward from the summit, as it strips snow away and leaves black rocky faces.

In winter cold air settles over the Tibetan Plateau, causing the formation of a low pressure system with a cyclonic or counter-clockwise airflow in the upper atmosphere at altitudes of about 9000 metres. This colder air over Tibet contrasts with the warmer air over India, giving rise to contrasting horizontal pressures; that is, low pressure over Tibet and high pressure over India. South of the Himalayas a west-to-east flowing jet stream is established, and dry winter weather prevails over India. In April the Tibetan Plateau usually starts to warm up, and as the air over Tibet continues to become warmer than the air over India, the horizontal temperature and pressures between the two countries are reversed from what they were in winter. This gives rise to a high pressure system with anticyclonic or clockwise circulation in the upper atmosphere which helps to establish an east-west flowing airstream, bringing summer monsoon rain to India and Nepal.

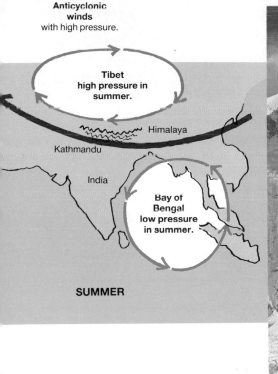

Anticyclonic winds with high pressure.

Tibet high pressure in summer.

Himalaya

Kathmandu

India

Bay of Bengal low pressure in summer.

SUMMER

In summer the jet stream is reversed and blows gently from the east, so that monsoon snow adheres to the mountains, giving them a wintry appearance.

49

Cottonwool wisps grow rapidly into billowing clouds which rise up the face of the Nuptse/Lhotse wall. Although summer mornings are often clear to begin with, monsoon clouds quickly form, and hide the peaks for most of the day.

Khumbu Climate

The climate of the Khumbu is dominated by the presence of the Himalaya. The high mountains deflect much of the dry cold winds which would otherwise blow south off the central Asian land-mass; and more significantly, they capture and hold the northward-moving monsoon along the southern face. The monsoon is not itself a rain, but a wind that carries rain. Originating in the Indian Ocean, it flows water-laden across India to rise up the slopes of the mountains, expanding and cooling as it ascends. Eventually the water vapour condenses and the rain pours down in torrents, mainly on the southern and middle slopes of the mountains. Because of their elevation, the high Himalaya provide a perpetual repository for these monsoon rains in the form of snow and glaciers, which continue to feed the rivers throughout the dry season.

As summer approaches, the monsoon moves up from the Bay of Bengal, usually reaching Khumbu about mid-June. Once established, the monsoon weather pattern is typically one of clear or partially clear mornings, with rapidly forming clouds enveloping the peaks and completely filling the valleys by midday. The mist becomes a damp drizzle and then, as the day progresses, it turns to heavy rain by nightfall. Sometimes days or even weeks of clinging mist with no sunshine at all are experienced.

This pattern continues until mid-September when the monsoon starts to withdraw.

Summer ends and with the approach of winter
temperatures in higher regions start to fall.
The monsoon can linger on however, with
quite heavy snowfalls down to 5000 metres.
Here the Khumbu Glacier and lake at Gorak
Shep are blanketed with an end-of-monsoon
snow fall.

There is little noticeable wind during the monsoon period, although there is an east-west flow in the upper atmosphere, but as winter approaches again the jet stream is reversed and the cold, dry westerly winds recommence. This change in wind direction is very noticeable on the highest peaks such as Everest and Lhotse, which sport banners of wind-driven snow cloud to the east, from October until June. The peaks quickly lose their snowy appearance and resume a black rocky character as the snow melts off the south faces or is blown away by the strong winds.

Once the winter is established it brings clear skies and sunny days from October to December. Temperatures drop steadily as the weeks progress, and heavy frosts from late October onwards freeze the ground at Namche Bazar to a depth of 45 centimetres. Occasional light snowfalls do occur in autumn but these usually melt quickly. The coldest months are December, January and February, and heavy falls of snow can come once the shortest day has passed. With the near zero temperatures the snow will then lie on the ground for weeks.

From January until late March the weather pattern is usually one of long clear periods, often of two to three weeks, interspersed with short intervals of unsettled weather which rarely lasts more than two to three days.

On average, from November to March temperatures at Namche Bazar do not rise more than a few degrees above zero during the day, and can drop as low as minus 12 degrees C. at night. The higher the altitude the lower the temperature will be. Minus 20 degrees C. or more is common at Lobuche.

During March and April the temperatures start to rise again, although there are still frosts and the possibility of an occasional late snowfall. May is often quite hot and brings an increase of pre-monsoon cloud with a few showers of rain, but these barely dampen the ground. The cycle is then repeated again with the onset of the next monsoon.

Annual precipitation averages about 1000mm, with 75% of it falling during the summer monsoon period. The high peaks receive most of their snow during this time and take on a winter-like appearance with snow falling to about 5500 metres. Quite heavy snowfalls often occur before the last of the monsoon withdraws from about mid-September, when temperatures in the higher regions start to drop rapidly.

Like a stalagmite a formation of ice has grown from water dripping off a curtain of icicles. Winter sunshine is warm enough to melt the icicles but in shaded areas and at night, low temperatures refreeze the water droplets as they land.

Threads of Nature

Deep in shadows, the narrow forested gorges contrast with steep rocky hillsides and grassy slopes of the upper valleys which are open to sun and wind. Above are the glaciers, snowfields, and towering peaks. This varied topography provides a wide diversity of habitats for many plant and animal species.

The topography of Nepal varies enormously from the flat and tropical Terai at only 150 metres above sea level to the icy peaks of Khumbu, culminating at the highest point on earth. From its low point of 3000 metres, the land within the Park rises another 5800 metres in altitude, encompassing a wide range of topography: deep narrow forested gorges, high grassy valleys, broad glaciated regions, and steep rocky mountainsides.

The Park can be roughly divided into three zones, governed mainly by altitude. These are a forested lower zone, a middle zone of alpine scrub, and an upper alpine zone. Within these zones is a variety of habitats in which wildlife is found. The vegetation varies according to its location and site as well as altitude.

The plant, bird, insect and animal species of the Park are also restricted in variety by these high altitudes. Many of the birds are migratory or come in summer only. Animal species are those which have adapted to thin air and cold temperatures. The butterflies and other insects are those whose pupae can withstand the long, cold winter months, the adults emerging once the temperatures have risen sufficiently.

Because many of the animals, insects and birds are dependent on the vegetation as a food source, they are usually found where that supply is best. In turn, the birds which feed on the insects will also be more concentrated where their food supply is greater. Predatory birds and animals range over wider domains in search of their prey, showing less preference for hunting sites, although breeding places are carefully chosen.

The land and its inhabitants are all tied inextricably together in a delicate balance which is easily upset. Without the forest and scrub the animals, birds and insects which live there will have no home or food supply. The predators would then be deprived of many of their food sources and would have only those creatures to prey on which were able to inhabit a treeless terrain, making their survival more precarious.

Destruction of the forests and scrub zones has a far reaching effect, causing erosion. At first, for five or more years there is no obvious change, but as the tree and shrub roots rot, the soil and rocks are no longer held together. With their network of support lost the rocks and soil are free to move, either loosened by frosts, then washed down by monsoon rains, or blown away by the wind. The balance is held by delicate threads, and if only one is cut the rest may fail also.

Key: Birch Trees   Juniper Trees   Blue Pines   Rhododendron Fir

The topography of Nepal varies enormously from the flat and tropical Terai at only 150 metres above sea level to the icy peaks of Khumbu, culminating at the highest point on earth.

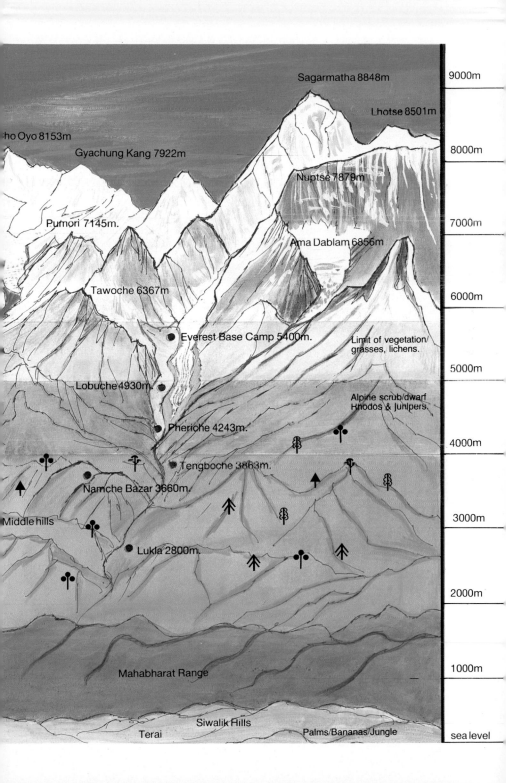

The Strongest Thread

The plants of Sagarmatha are its lifeline, supporting communities of wildlife in a demanding environment in one of the extreme habitats on Earth. Because Nepal occupies the central sector of the vast Himalayan mountain chain, and sits astride the cross-roads of several botanical provinces, such as the Sino-Japanese, the Indo-Malayan, and the Western and Central Asiatic, its plant life tends to be representative of all of these areas. In addition many plants native to western Europe and North America are also found in the alpine regions, because the Himalaya acts as a 'climatic corridor' for plant migration. Being situated at the eastern end of the long Himalaya, the Park is more affected by the monsoon, receiving more rain than western districts of Nepal. High peaks to the south, however, also cause a slight rain shadow effect with reduced rainfall. This influences the composition of its vegetation, which is characteristic of many of the inner drier valleys of Nepal. With increases in altitude the vegetation zones change from predominantly forest, to scrub, then to grasses, mosses and lichens until an altitude is reached where all vegetation ceases to survive.

A dry climate is reflected in the vegetation. Although the Park is at the eastern end of the Himalaya, which receives more rain than the west, high peaks to the south deflect much of the monsoon rain, and little falls over the upper valleys.

(Opposite): Gouged by an ancient glacier which was once much larger than at present, the U shaped valley beneath Mt. Kantaiga has clearly marked zones of vegetation. Trees of the lower forest levels give way to shrubs in the alpine scrub zone, and with increases in altitude these dwindle and disappear too, until only grasses, mosses and lichens survive.

Forests. The forested areas in Sagarmatha National Park are not large, and were probably never much more extensive than at present. Increased demands for firewood in recent times have thinned these forests at an alarming rate. The main tree species are blue pine, junipers, silver fir, rhododendrons and birch, the last three often occuring together.

Most visitors enter the Park at its lowest point, 2800 metres in the Dudh Kosi valley, at the village of Monjo. As befits the highest National Park in the world, this approach is dramatic and impressive. The dominant forest tree here is the Blue Himalayan Pine with its drooping, elegant, five-needled foliage and banana-shaped pendulous cones. It clothes the valley sides and clings in scattered colonies to the soaring cliffs, persisting northwards up the river gorges of the Dudh Kosi and the Bhote Kosi to an altitude of approximately 3500 metres. Known to the Sherpas as *metang*, the Blue Pine is the fastest growing tree in the Park, with growth rates of up to twenty-two metres in fifty years. Its timber is often used in house construction, and because it exudes an inflammable resin, strips are hacked from the bases of trees to provide torches for night-time travellers.

Associated with the pine are many trees and shrubs which are readily seen in most comparable altitudes in Nepal. *Rhododendron arboreum*, the national flower of Nepal, abounds in various shades of red and pink, but the more scarce white form is also frequently seen. This species has the same wide altitude tolerance as the Blue Himalayan Pine and can be seen on the upper parts of the ridge which leads to Tengboche Monastery.

In the Monjo area there are occasional shrubs of the green-yellow flowered rhododendron with its characteristic mahogany-coloured peeling bark. The 'Lily of the Valley' bush *(Pieris formosa)* grows in abundance here, with trees of Himalayan Hemlock *(Tsuga dumosa)*, Wallich's Yew *(Taxus wallichiaha)*, and Himalayan Oak *(Quercus semicarpifolia)*.

On the forest floor are the Small Leaved Cotoneaster and the Scaly Rhododendron. Both these dwarf species of the shrub layer are also plants with a very wide tolerance and can be found in various forms and sub-species up to the higher wind-blasted alpine levels of 4500 metres and more.

The Himalayan Vine romps twentyfive metres high in the crowns of trees, or up sheer rock faces, and turns into a cascade of scarlet foliage in mid-October, while in spring the Mountain Clematis showers the branches of its host trees in a flurry of white. In the autumn the Campbell's Maple turns bright gold, and the silvery-green leaves of the Himalayan Whitebeam shrivel to a gleaming white in the dry post-monsoon air.

Another imposing conifer of the Park is the Silver Fir, locally known as *tashing*, which extends from about 3300 metres in the Dudh Kosi gorge up to about 4250 metres on the more sheltered slopes of the high inner valleys of the Bhote Kosi, Dudh Kosi and Imja Khola. With the gleaming, silvery undersurface of its needle-like leaves and its upright, candlestick-like cones, this species is an attractive and often dominant tree of the upper forest levels. It has growth rates of up to ten and a half metres in fifty years, at altitudes of around 3200 metres near Phunki Tenga, but at higher altitudes, around Khumbjung, Khunde and Tengboche, it only reaches heights of up to nine metres in the same time.

A mosaic of form and colour, the forested slopes beneath Mt. Ama Dablam are a mixture of juniper, rhododendron, birch and fir trees. Approaching winter has already turned birch leaves yellow, and given the barberry in the left foreground a red tinge.

An equally characteristic and dominant tree of the sub-alpine regions is the Himalayan Birch. Known to the Sherpas as *takpa*, it is of considerable economic use to them. When seen as a mature forest, with the peeling amber- coloured bark back-lit by low warm sunlight, and the grey-green lichen *Usnea* blowing like tattered flags from its limbs in the alpine breeze, then the true beauty of this lovely tree can be fully appreciated.

A magnificent birch forest stands on the lower, northeast-facing flanks of Tamserku, whilst immediately across the river, the steep slopes which lead up to Tengboche are dominated by a mixture of silver fir, tree and shrub rhododendrons and various species of juniper. Juniper wood and foliage, called *sukpa* by the Sherpas, is burned in the temples and used as an incense by the Buddhist monks. Perhaps the finest mature example of the tree juniper are adjacent to the gompas of some villages, where they reach a height of fifteen metres or more. These are exceptional though, and must be very old as the juniper is a slow growing tree. Others growing around Khunde and Khumbjung have reached a height of just over four metres in fifty years, and almost eight metres within the warmer valley environment of Phunki Tenga.

The rhododendrons are mixed with birch and silver fir and do not usually occur in pure stands. The red-flowered tree rhododendron *(Rhododendron arboreum)* which occurs on the sunnier south side of the ridge leading to Tengboche, gives way at higher altitudes to the pink, mauve or white-flowered varieties of *Rhododendron wallichii,* and *R. campylocarpum* with its delicate lemon-yellow bells. These are common in the shadier forested areas north of Tengboche. On the cooler side of the ridge below Tengboche, above the Imja Khola, are a few of the large-leaved *Rhododendron hodgsonii* which bear beautiful magenta flowers. Although abundant further east in Nepal they are not common in the Park.

Papery, amber-coloured flakes of bark peel from the trunks of birch trees, as if they were shedding their skins.

Like shredded cloth, weathered by wind and rain, *Usnea* lichen hanging in tatters from the limbs of birch trees is highlighted by sunlight filtering through the forest.

Rhododendron campylocarpum

Rhododendron arboreum

Rhododendron wallichii

Rhododendron arboreum

Lower Alpine Scrub. The Lower Alpine Scrub Zone is where the mixed forest of birch, fir and tree rhododendrons fades out, and the dominant vegetation of the mountainside becomes alpine scrub. The characteristic features of this zone are the shrubby Alpine Cinquefoil, dwarf rhododendrons, dwarf junipers, Sikkim Willow, *Cassiope fastigiata*, and dwarf cotoneasters.

Among the shelter afforded by this shrub complex, a wealth of herbaceous or sub-herbaceous alpine plants can be found growing. The alpine gentians bloom in the autumn, while the Himalayan Edelweiss flowers during the monsoon alongside *Codonopsis thalictrifolia*, *Thalictrum chelidonii*, the Nepalese Lily and its other bulbous relatives such as *Notholirium macrophyllum* and *Fritillaria cirrhosa*. Himalayan primroses abound: *Primula denticulata* with its spherical flower heads in varying shades of mauve is common in the more open glades, the delicate, purple *Primula atrodentata* hides in the lee of overhanging rocks, violet *Primula woolastonii* perches on the moss-covered brows of stony ledges, and the tall yellow *Primula sikkimensis* thrives in the wet lush areas of streamsides.

Rhododendron setosum

Small-leaved cotoneaster

Alpine cinquefoil.

Primula sikkimensis

Like miniature trees the shrub rhododendrons, junipers and cotoneasters, Sikkim Willow and cinquefoils grow in abundance in the lower alpine scrub zone. Sheltering beneath their low branches other herbaceous plants wait out the long cold winter, ready to burst into flower when summer arrives.

Primula denticulata

65

Upper Alpine Zone. With an increase in altitude into the Upper Alpine Zone the shrub layer diminishes and changes as the climate becomes colder and drier. The dwarf rhododendron species dwindle in variety until the sole representative above 5000 metres is the Snow Rhododendron *(R. nivale)* which hugs the savage slopes to escape the dessicating effects of the mountain winds. Other dwarf shrubs common in these dry valley uplands include the Himalayan Buckthorn, and the Alpine Shrubby Horsetail, the seemingly ever-present Black Juniper and Shrubby Cinquefoil. Associated herbs include the Ornate Gentian, Przwalskis Mountain Gentian, Edelweiss, and the Spiny Mountain Poppy.

Above this zone, and up as far as the permanent snow line at about 5750 metres, plant life is restricted to lichens, mosses, dwarf grasses and sedges, alpine cresses, and the 'cushion plants' such as *Arenaria polytrichioides*, and the white woolly *Tanacetum gossypinum*.

Ephemeral plant life has been recorded as high as 6000 metres amongst the morainic debris at the base of cliffs in the Western Cwm of Sagarmatha; but this is exceptional, and it is generally accepted that permanent life ceases at about 5750 metres.

Swathed in cobweb-like fibres, the strange *Saussurea gossypiphora* maintains its own micro-climate around itself, and is able to withstand the temperature extremes of a moraine habitat.

One of the most beautiful of Himalayan plants, the Blue Poppy derives its name, *Meconopsis horridula,* from an armoury of straw-coloured spikes which protrude from the leaves and stems.

Delicate blooms flourish in a demanding high altitude environment. Small leathery leaves, hairiness, a mat or cushion form, and an ability to flower and seed quickly are some adaptations which enable these plants to survive in what seem to be impossible growing conditions.

Snow-capped, Tawoche's summit rises above radiating shoulders. Vegetation in these upper zones dwindles from dwarf shrubs to cushion plants, grasses, mosses and lichens, until even they cease to survive in the savage elements of wind and cold.

Seasonal Changes

During the greater part of the year, October to April, when there is little precipitation and temperatures can be very low, not much is seen of the multitude of plants hiding in the dusty earth. The tree rhododendron leaves hang down, their sides rolled in against the dessicating effects of the cold air, giving them a half dead appearance; the birch trees are leafless, and other shrubby plants look lifeless. The small leaves of the dwarf rhododendrons are a drab brown colour, blending them into the dry, brown slopes where even the grass is only a short stubble.

About mid April the ground takes on a faint sheen of green as the new grass starts to grow. Barberry bushes produce new, bright green leaves and their first yellow flowers begin to appear. Close to the ground, small purple irises spring up, red spearheads of euphorbia and the first green rosettes of new primula leaves push quickly through the hard soil. By the time the rhododendrons start to bloom in early May, primulas are flowering and briar roses sport deep pink or cream blooms. Forests take on a green hue again as birch trees produce new leaves, and upper slopes are tinged with the pink and yellow of rhododendron flowers.

When the first monsoon rains come in mid-June there is a sudden rush of plant growth. Hillsides become grassy and dotted with tiny violet vetches, bright yellow cinquefoils and pink orchid-like *Roscoea alpina*, while dainty pink heads of *Androsace* cluster on banks and terraces.

The higher alpine meadows, up to 5000 metres, are brilliantly hued by yellow buttercups and purple aster daisies, cerise clusters of *Pedicularis* and pale pink spikes of *Polygonum* species, and the grasses flourish. Even the moraines are adorned with the fragile sky-blue flowers of poppies and the hardier gentians. Edelweiss star the slopes with white and the Snow Rhododendron tinges them with lavender. Although many of these flowers seem too delicate to survive the harsh environment in which they live, they have all adapted to it in some way.

This floral spectacle continues until mid September, with different species coming into flower every week. Then the monsoon starts to withdraw. Temperatures are still mild but growth stops and plants rapidly die off. Only the blue gentians still flower. The tall heads of euphorbia quickly turn scarlet and within a week brown and wither. The first week in October gives bright red barberry, yellow and gold birch trees and sees the drying grasses disappearing as the ever hungry cattle make the most of available food.

With the return of winter there are dry, dusty slopes again, twiggy shrubs and bare trees, with only the dark green firs, blue pines, rhododendrons and other evergreen shrubs showing any foliage. This is the scene most visitors see, for few come to Khumbu during the summer when monsoon rains make the plants vibrant with colour.

In summer the tiny Snow Rhododendron *(R. nivale)* colours whole hillsides with its mauve blooms. A trekkers' camp set among these beautiful flowers, at 5000 metres in the Imja Valley, looks across to Island Peak and the soaring wall of Nuptse and Lhotse.

Spring, summer and winter bring vivid contrasts in the overall colour of the landscape, clearly shown in these views of Mendelphu Hill above Namche Bazar.

Monsoon moisture produces the vivid green lush growth, but even before the rains cease for the year many plants are dying back as they anticipate the coming of winter. The orange patches on the left side of the hill are *euphorbia* which has turned red, and within a week will be brown and withered.

The driest time is early spring when everything is dust brown after almost five months without rain.

Winter brings a white mantle for a few weeks only each year. Because of the cold temperatures, snow which falls is very light and dry, providing little moisture when it melts.

Warm summer rains bring renewed life, and alpine meadows blossom into flamboyant colour.

One of the first to appear each spring, the flower of *Iris kumaonensis* is almost as big as its leaves.

Ripe barberries provide a splash of colour and food for many birds in autumn.

The last flowers to appear each summer, *Gentiana depressa* often persists well into autumn when all other plants have withdrawn for winter.

Orchid-like *Roscoea alpina* is a member of the Ginger family. It appears with the first summer rains and has a brief flowering season.

71

Links in a Chain — The Animals

Linked with the plants are the animal inhabitants. Each is a separate link in the food chain, yet bound to each other by the threads of the 'web of life'; each is dependent on some other form of life for its existence.

In common with the rest of the Nepal Himalaya, Sagarmatha is not over endowed with animal species, and most visitors will be lucky to see any as they walk the main trekking routes. Away from the main routes, and during early morning or evening hours, the chances of seeing something are much higher. This lack of animals is apparently a result of the geologically recent origin of the Himalaya and other evolutionary factors. The other main factor in the reduction of wild animal numbers is the presence over the years of humans and their grazing animals, which have depleted forest and scrub areas, altering the habitats of many creatures.

Reptiles and Amphibians: It is not surprising that reptiles are rare in the high Himalaya, with the cold temperatures experienced for most of the year. Being cold-blooded animals, the snakes, geckos and skinks rely on warmth from the sun to vitalise their body tissues. This warmth is not available at high altitudes.

A few species of keelback snakes live up to 3650 metres and, although not yet recorded in the Park, possibly occur in the lower fringes or in the valley on the approaches from Lukla. The commonest and most widely distributed is the Striped Keelback. This conspicuous snake has an olive-brown back with black spots intersected by yellow or buff-coloured stripes, and an unusually long tail.

The Wolf Snake is also common in forests throughout the hills. It is a small, dark brown snake with yellowish crossbars and an elongated, flattened, pear-shaped head. Both the Wolf Snake and the Striped Keelback are harmless to humans.

Two species of pit vipers, the Mountain Pit Viper and the Himalayan Pit Viper, have been recorded at high altitudes and could occur in the Park. All Pit Vipers have narrow necks, triangular heads and eyes with vertical pupils. They are named for the deep pits which lie on each side of the head, between the nostrils and the eyes. The venom of pit vipers affects red blood cells and causes some haemorrhaging. Although a bite is painful, the venom is not deadly to humans.

Probably only one species of skink, *Scincella sikimensis*, occurs in the Park. About eight to nine centimetres long, it has a bronzey-brown back marked with irregular dark brown or black spots. The sides are a darker brown and the belly is either whitish or a pale colour. The common Garden Lizard, a rough-scaled creature with a spiny dorsal ridge, might also be seen in lower-altitude regions. Males have a bright red head during the breeding season.

Three species of frogs are likely to occur. *Rana liebigii*, a variable greyish to reddish-brown frog, is often eaten by hill peoples. The two other species are *Rana polunini*, an olive-green frog which inhabits small streams, and *Rana sikimensis*. The latter is greenish to reddish-brown with a dark brown V-shaped mark on top of its head. The tree frog *Polypedates maculatus* possibly occurs also. Like all toads, this dark-coloured species has a dry, warty skin and behind each eye a gland which produces a milky poison.

Ready to bound away at any hint of danger, a group of Himalayan Tahr watches an intruder from the comparative safety of height. Usually found on steep rocky hillsides well above the treeline, they will descend to lower levels in spring, in search of food.

Frogs have teeth on the upper jaw only. Two species which live at high altitudes are the most likely to be found. A search of damp places and around springs particularly in summer will most likely reveal these amphibians.

Mammals. The variety of mammal species which are definitely known to occur, or should be found in the Park, is however reasonably large, and includes moles, shrews, rodents, hares, mustelids, cats, deer, monkeys, bears, cattle and canines. Their habitats vary in altitude and include streamside or wet places, bamboo forest, birch/rhododendron/fir forest, steep rocky mountainsides, open grassy hillsides, and high, bouldery, open-type terrain such as moraines. The lower forested areas provide warmth and shelter but the upper slopes of mountains are bleak and inhospitable with extremes of temperature, strong winds and shortages of water. The strong winds blow snow into deep drifts and cover the ground. Water, although present, is often frozen as ice or snow and is unavailable. At high altitudes there are also physiological problems caused by reduced atmospheric pressure; animals living there must have bodies adapted to surviving on less oxygen and in fluctuating temperatures. Larger mammals that range above the tree line have very thick coats which help them to retain body heat, and some, such as the marmot, have a compact form with shortened limbs which also helps to reduce loss of body heat.

At high altitudes the sun's rays lose less heat to the air as they pass through the thinner atmosphere. This causes the temperature near the ground to be higher than the surrounding air temperature, and it is this microclimate which allows some plants and smaller animals to survive. Some mammals such as pikas and marmots live underground in burrows or cavities where there is a microclimate much warmer than that outside. Another adapation which helps them to survive is their gregarious habit, and a preference for living in large colonies.

Long whiskers twitching and ears alert, the tiny Pika, or Mouse Hare, surveys for danger before venturing out to forage for grasses which it will store for winter use. At the slightest alarm it will vanish beneath the boulders, where numerous runways and tunnels allow it to live in comparative warmth and safety.

An inhabitant of the lower forests, particularly in areas of bamboo, is the Red or Lesser Panda. Sometimes called the Catbear, because of its size, the Red Panda is a bright chestnut colour with a round white face and large ears. Its coat is thick, with dark brown underparts, and its long bushy tail is ringed with bars of white. Of nocturnal habits, it usually spends the day roosting in the topmost branches of trees, then browses on leaves and fruit from dusk to dawn. It has a sixth finger, a pad on the front paw that helps it to grasp stems when it is feeding. The Red Panda seems to have little in common with either bears or the Giant Panda whose home is in the bamboo forests of south-west China, but both pandas do have several similarities.

A number of mammals will only be found in the lower altitudes of the Park and these include two insectivores — the Short Tailed Mole and shrews. Moles have small eyes, short ears, and fore-limbs which have been modified for digging and burrowing. Shrews are long-nosed, rat-like mammals with poor vision, and owing to their nocturnal habits are not usually seen by trekkers. Species of shrew which are likely to be found are the Brown-toothed Shrew, Tibetan and Himalayan Water Shrews, and Musk Shrew. The Brown-toothed Shrews live in damp places at the edges of evergreen rhododendron and conifer forests, or wet alpine meadows near streams where there is a rich litter layer and plenty of moss and grass; while the Water Shrews prefer clear streamsides flowing through the forests.

Bats are another nocturnal mammal unlikely to be noticed but possibly found in the lower regions of the Park. The Leaf-nosed Bat, an insect eater, is common throughout Nepal at around 3000 metres in altitude, and the Short-nosed Fruit Bat or Flying Fox occurs at up to 3600 metres. As its name suggests, it feeds on fruit.

The Himalayan Black Bear is distributed throughout Nepal with resident bears in the Khumbu. These large mammals which may grow to over one and a half metres and weigh up to 230 kilograms, have a black coat with a distinct white chevron marking on the chest. They hibernate during the winter months in caves or the nooks of trees, not to avoid the cold but because of a shortage of food. During this time all their bodily functions — digestion, heartbeat and respiration are so greatly reduced that they retain most of their weight during the four or five months of hibernation. In the summer months they raid crops to obtain food, showing little fear of man whom they have been known to attack, although visitors are unlikely to come in contact with them.

Within the birch and rhododendron forest, the Musk Deer hides away. This shy, diminutive deer stands about fiftysix centimetres at the shoulder and weighs between twelve and fifteen kilograms. It has a frizzled coat varying in colour between grey and brown, depending on the season. Unlike other deer, Musk Deer do not produce antlers. Instead, the buck has extremely long canine teeth projecting from the upper jaw. These are used for territorial combat and defence and assist in removing mosses and lichens from rocks and trees in the winter months. Grasses make up a large proportion of the summer diet. The male Musk Deer has a gland in his abdomen that secretes a pungent musk which is highly valued by the perfumery and oriental-medicine trades. In the past, and still to a limited extent today, this supported a lucrative poaching trade. It is for this reason that the species has been hunted to the point where its survival has become endangered.

Small currant-like droppings are an indication of the presence of musk deer and it is known that they defecate at certain places, probably to indicate territorial rights. The females and young live in small groups whereas the males usually live solitary lives except during the breeding season. Gestation of young is about five months (160 days) and usually one fawn is born between April and June.

Several other animals found in the Park are known to be predators of the Musk Deer. The commonest of these are the wolves, jackals and wild dogs, although foxes and large birds of prey will also take the young.

The Mountain Fox is a forest dweller and is occasionally seen slinking quietly away into the trees. It is typically fox-like in appearance, with a superb brush and long, chestnut to rufous coloured fur. Being a predator, it steals from the nests of ground birds as well as taking the young of the musk deer.

The Yellow-throated Marten and North Indian Marten are large ferret-like mustelids which prey on other small animals inhabiting the forested or semi-forested areas. They are known to hunt the Musk Deer in pairs, chasing their prey until it becomes exhausted. The North Indian Marten has a black head, hindquarters and tail.

Although Sagarmatha National Park is at high altitudes, and monkeys are thought of as creatures of tropical forests, two species are found in the Dudh Kosi Valley and may extend their range into the Park. These are the Rhesus monkey, commonly found around the temples in Kathmandu, as well as forests up to 3000 metres, and the Common Langur. The Langur are large brownish-grey monkeys with distinctive white heads and black faces, and they inhabit cold conifer forests up to 3660 metres.

The Himalayan Wolf prefers the upper forest limits where the trees give way to alpine scrub. It presents the greatest threat to the livestock of the local people, especially in the high summer pastures where it frequently kills young cattle. The Wolf has a brush-like tail, and its thick cream-grey coat, which is almost wool-like in texture, provides protection against the cold. Large teeth in a heavy muzzle allow it to easily kill smaller animals. It is not unusual to see this animal or to find the trail of a lone wolf crossing snow-covered 6000 metre passes as they wander in search of new territory.

The dog-like Jackal is more often heard howling than seen. Varying in colour from yellow and reds to browns and greys, it has short legs and a long body. Jackals approach villages during the night to scavenge, a practice which causes a frenzy of defensive barking from domestic dogs. It is thought that their numbers have increased within the Khumbu since deforestation has made conditions more suitable for them.

Steep, inaccessible cliffs and crags of the upper treeline are the home of the Himalayan Tahr, a species of wild goat. In the spring they are lured to relatively low levels by new growth and are often seen on the trail between Namche and Phunki Tenga and on the cliffs of the Dudh Kosi near Phunki Tenga and Phortse. These powerful animals stand about a metre at the shoulder, with males displaying a magnificent yellow mane during the winter months when mating takes place. They have large curling horns, and move agilely in groups across the steep rock faces while grazing available grasses. Males and females remain apart until late summer to rejoin in autumn. The mating season begins in winter with fighting between the males, and the young are born in May and June. As the Tahr is a goat, it can interbreed with domestic species.

Above the treeline where the landscape is harsher and dominated by small shrubs, grasses and lichens, the animal most often seen is the Pika or

Himalayan Mouse Hare. Similar to a guinea pig in form and habit, they are found among the large boulders or rock slides and glacial moraines where there are many spaces for runways and nesting chambers. During the warm days prior to winter they can be seen around the broken slopes above the fresh water springs at Lobuche and on the trail above Pheriche. Insulated and camouflaged by their dense grey-brown fur, they are particularly well adapted to survive the extreme cold. The soles of their feet are also furred, enabling them to move over smooth rocks. Instead of hibernating they live on the grasses that they have collected and stored during the summer months.

The Woolly Himalayan Hare is another inhabitant of the upper grassy areas. Like all hares, it has long ears and strong hind legs for running. The young hares (called leverets), are born with hair and are able to see. True rabbits are not known in Nepal.

The Park has several families of rodents, the commonest being the House Rat and House Mouse whose habitat and form need no description. Less common is the Alpine Vole which lives in forests and breeds in the hollows of decayed trees, making a nest of grass to protect its young.

The Himalayan Marmot, a rodent, is found from 4200 to 5500 metres, making it the highest living mammal in the world. Its fur is a light yellow, a good camouflage colour which blends into its surroundings of dry grasses and earth. The Marmot lives in burrows and feeds on available vegetation. Like other marmots it gives a shrill whistling call when alarmed.

Although the Snow Leopard has not been sighted in the Khumbu for some years, it is hoped that it is still present. This beautiful cat is slightly smaller than the common leopard, with a longer tail, and a coat of soft grey to pure white, starred with pale rosettes. Its habitat ranges from about 2000 metres in winter to 5500 metres in summer. It is known to mate in winter, and after a gestation period of 93 to 99 days a litter of between two and four cubs is born in spring.

The Yak and the female (Nak) are a common sight around the Park. Although the Yak is now domesticated in the Khumbu, wild ones are still thought to live in the border regions of Nepal and Tibet. Its thick matted coat, large lungs, and rasp-like tongue which allows it to lick moisture from the high alpine grasses, are adapatations which allow it to survive extremely well in the thin, cold air of high altitudes. Being vulnerable to diseases it does not adapt well to lower altitudes, and only in winter is it taken below 3000 metres. A fully grown bull can weigh up to 550 kilograms and stands two metres at the shoulder. Commonly used domestic crossbreeds are called *zum* (cow) and *zopkiok* (bull).

Last but not least is the Yeti or Abominable Snowman. This creature of legend and myth has evoked much popular and scientific interest although its existence has yet to be proved. It has been mentioned in the song written by the Tibetan mystic, Milarepa (1038 — 1120 A.D.); and a Bavarian, John Schitsherger, recorded in 1472 the presence of a strange fur-covered man that lived in the high mountains of Mongolia. Chinese and Mongolian books of the 18th and 19th centuries describe similar creatures which are said to live in Tibet, and a painting at Tengboche monastery depicts the Yeti.

Backward curling horns and a long shaggy coat distinguish the Yak from other crossbreeds. Once roaming wild, but now domesticated, the yaks have proved to be invaluable to the Sherpas because of an ability to survive at high altitudes.

The Sherpas distinguish three different types of Yeti. First is *Drema* or *Telma*, a stout man-like ape with grey or reddish fur. It is considered to be the messenger of calamities. Second is *Chuti* which appears as a huge bear and preys on goats, sheep and yaks, killing them by seizing their horns and twisting the victim's head. The third is known as *Mite* or *Midre*. It has reddish or golden fur and a forehead covered with long hair. It walks upright and attacks animals and sometimes men.

First reports were by a C.W. Waddell in 1898 who found a trail of 'the hairy wild man'. Since then several expeditions to the Himalaya have reported finding mysterious footprints in the snow, but nothing more. All the footprints described are large, with toes and a thumb-like depression on each foot. They are much larger than that of a human, and all have a characteristic big toe separated from the remaining toes. When reported sightings are followed up, it usually transpires that the story teller has not actually seen the Yeti himself.

To substantiate the claims that an unknown creature does exist, there have been several bizarre incidents. Mountaineering expeditions have heard high-pitched whistles, and their camps have been visited at night. In 1974 the Japanese, and in 1980 the Polish, found that something had left telltale footprints around their tents. When members began following and photographing them they were screamed at by an unseen creature. In 1974, a Sherpa girl also claimed to have been attacked by a large ape-like creature, and several yaks' necks were broken by something which had grabbed them by the horns and twisted their necks.

One day perhaps the existence of the Yeti will be proved and, like China's Giant Panda and Africa's Mountain Gorilla it will no longer be only a legend.

Left; The fearsome yeti lurking in the mountains around Sagarmatha is depicted in many traditional paintings.

Above; Facial markings and a ringed, bushy tail give the Red or Lesser Panda a racoon-like appearance.

Middle; Snapping thin branches as if they were twigs, a Himalayan Black Bear strips a tree for new spring leaves.

Above; An inhabitant of remote mountain areas, the Snow Leopard has been hunted in the past for its superb coat, and is now an endangered species.

Left; Checking for possible danger, a Himalayan Marmot pauses at the entrance to its burrow before venturing out.

79

The Birds

At least 118 species of birds find food and shelter within the variety of habitats found in Sagarmatha National Park. These include resident birds, summer nesters, winter visitors and migrants. Their habitats are similar to those of the animals but also include others of a minor nature such as dwarf bamboo stands, village fields and hedges, stream and riversides.

At the confluence of the Bhote Kosi and Dudh Kosi rivers, where the wind funnels down the gorges between cold shaded cliffs, the jaunty, tail-cocking, White-capped River Chat and the slightly smaller Plumbeous Redstart are found. Both species range upwards along streams, the Redstart to as high as 3660 metres, and the River Chat to over 4880 metres in places such as Chukong, Gokyo and Lobuche. Spending most of their time near rivers and streams where they look for insect life, they are active birds and can often be seen running about after prey, leaping into the air if they notice an insect buzzing overhead. The Plumbeous Redstart occasionally supplements its diet with berries from nearby vegetation.

The Brown Dipper is another remarkable bird often seen near streams and rivers. The plumage of this species is a uniform brown but the dull feathers make up in waterproofing for what they lack in colour. A Dipper has an exceedingly large urogpygeal gland on the rump. While preening, oil from this organ is liberally spread over the feathers to prevent them from becoming soaked while the bird 'dips' in the frigid water.

As well as being 'waterproofed' Dippers also have an extremely dense layer of downy feathers to retain body warmth, and have lids which close over their nostrils to keep water out of the breathing passages. They are able to remain submerged for long periods, even in turbulent waters which appear unsuitable for bird life, swimming underwater using their wings as they do not have webbed feet. Whether or not they actually walk along the bottom of a pond has never been ascertained. This hardy species breeds late in winter and subsequently may ascend ice-fringed streams to over 4575 metres.

From the river the base of the south-facing slope stretching up to Namche is covered in pine trees. This is the habitat of the Long-tailed Minivet, one of the most colourful birds in the Park, the males with their red and black plumage, the females yellow and grey. The Minivet, with its frequent clear 'tweet, tweet' call is a summer visitor, and usually places its superb lichen-encrusted nest high in a tree.

In spring, a mournful and deliberate song, repeated in snatches, is often heard issuing from the blue pines near the trail ascending to Namche. This is the song of the Chestnut-bellied Rock Thrush. The male Rock Thrush has a beautiful blue head and back and can usually be seen sitting conspicuously on the tops of trees or on exposed branches. It is a medium-altitude species that just reaches within the southern rim of the Park.

Across the valley from this pine forest the steep north-facing slopes under Mt. Kwongde are covered with dwarf bamboo, the preferred territory of the White-browed Tit Babbler, a confiding species with a conspicuously marked face that peers at intruders from close range.

The extensive dwarf bamboo habitat of the southern edge of the Park may also harbour Parrotbills, fluffy-feathered babblers almost entirely restricted to bamboos. No Parrotbills have been seen in the Park, but this is probably due to a scarcity of investigators rather than a lack of birds.

Namche Bazar, the first large village reached in the Park, is the haunt of Snow Pigeons, attractive birds with largely white underparts and black heads. Snow Pigeons nest and roost in Khumbu cliffs but appear to spend most of their feeding time in Sherpa fields. While each individual pigeon is a fine sight in itself, the true magnificence of the species is appreciated only when an entire flock lifts off together, wheeling and turning in split-second synchrony, their underparts and white wing linings flashing in the sun as they bank across the face of a grand snow summit.

Hedges around Namche fields provide nesting sites and sheltering stations for the Beautiful Rose Finch and other small passerines. This finch, possibly the commonest bird in Khumbu, feeds in fields or grassy swards but immediately flits to the safety of a bush if a predator or intruder appears. While the male Beautiful Rose Finch sports a pale pink plumage, accentuated on the rump and underparts, it is the least brightly coloured Rose Finch in the Park, and when compared with its gaudy relatives, the Pink-browed Rose Finch or the Common Rose Finch, it could possibly be called the least beautiful. The brown female lacks outstanding markings and is one of the drabbest and most nondescript birds in Khumbu.

The national bird of Nepal, the Danphe or Impeyan Pheasant, is often seen around Namche, and with nine colours in its plumage, many of them iridescent, it is one of the finest birds of the upper forest levels. Impeyans live from about 3660 to 4880 metres, where they dig in fields and grassy openings for tubers and roots. They are among the noisiest birds in the Park, the males calling stridently from ledges and rock prominences. On spring mornings they often call before dawn as they warm to the day's routine which may include courtship flights, short, slow, parachute-like descents, with wings arched high and tail fanned to provide maximum impact on the blue-eye-shadowed females watching from slopes above.

Iridescent plumage gleams in early morning sunlight as male Danphe pheasants dig for tubers in a potato field. It is Nepal's national bird and the brilliant male has nine colours, whereas the female is an overall drab brown, with her only adornment a ring of blue around each eye.

81

After Namche the Everest trail crosses steep south-east facing slopes above the Dudh Kosi gorge where overgrazing and habitat misuse is evident. From here, looking down into the Dudh Kosi gorge, soaring Himalayan Griffons or even Lammergeiers are often seen. Viewing flying birds from above is a sensation rarely experienced but one that does happen frequently in the Sagarmatha region.

Himalayan Griffons are large birds, possibly the heaviest in the Park. They soar on wings that measure over two and a half metres from tip to tip, and soar they must if they are to gain altitude for they are too heavy to fly uphill. If trying to ascend before the sun has warmed the slopes, the birds will circle around and around with much flapping and gliding, expending prodigious amounts of energy with no results, only managing to maintain altitude but unable to climb. The birds must wait until draughts lift them up. Once airborne they ascend effortlessly on rising currents to well over 6100 metres, before setting their wings in gliding cross-country descents. They rest and nest on the cliffs of the Dudh Kosi and Bhote Kosi gorges appearing in large numbers around the Park. It seems that the high number of domestic animals favours the maintenance of a sizeable population of these scavengers.

The Lammergeier or Bearded Vulture also uses updraughts for ascending. This imposing bird, its head completely feathered and its yellow eyes staring from between red orbital rims, glides in graceful curves around the Khumbu cliffs. Its wingspan measures up to three metres in large males. Even in silhouette against the sky, the Lammergeier's long tail with a blunt-pointed tip readily distinguishes it from the Griffon. For its size, it is extremely agile, but it is a shy bird, neither venturing too close to humans nor contesting with Griffons the possession of carcasses. On the ground the long, slim Lammergeier is no match for the heavy aggressive Himalayan Griffon, but once both species take to the air Lammergeiers will circle well out of their way to attack a Griffon. In an aerial contest the Lammergeier is surprisingly quick, turning swiftly with great flaps to lunge at the harrassed Griffon. Contact may be made, as feathers sometimes fly, but the Griffon avoids the Lammergeier by diving rapidly out of the area with partly closed wings. Although never known to actually hunt prey, the Lammergeier can also be aggressive towards species other than Griffons.

There are also eagles in the Park, all of them smaller and faster than the Griffon or Lammergeier. The Golden Eagle, a species found from North America through Europe and northern Asia to the Himalaya, is the resident eagle of the Park, and frequently seen soaring near the great yellow cliffs that rise just above the main Everest trail, below and to the east of Khumbjung. The Golden Eagle is a killer of exceptional ability. When Impeyan Pheasants or Tibetan Snow Cocks see this predator, they leap into the air and dive screaming down an open slope, alerting the entire region to the eagles presence. To catch food the Golden Eagle must hunt making good use of surprise. When looking for a victim the eagle tightly hugs the steep slopes, then upon cresting a rise will suddenly pounce upon any prey feeding in the open. In this way it secures large game birds and small mammals, possibly including the occasional young Himalayan Tahr. Another Golden Eagle hunting style is the direct long-range dive. It is estimated from observations that in one of these dives they will attack from distances of up to one kilometre to surprise their victim.

While the Golden Eagle remains as a year round resident in the Park, the Steppe or Nepal Eagle occurs here only on migration. Many transitory birds appear in the Park, but the routes used for migration are poorly understood. The 1960 Indian Everest Expedition found three of these birds dead on the South Col, at 7896 metres, one of the specimens being carried down for identification. So far this constitutes the highest known altitude recorded for the Steppe Eagle.

There is a small possibility that the Steppe Eagle's migration route lies across the South Col but it is more likely that the birds found there were caught in a hurricane force wind — the type that frequently blows about these giant mountains — and were deposited there against their will. There are many places where the main chain of mountains dips to 6000 metres or lower, such as the Nangpa La, Lho La, and Nup La, which are more likely to serve as migration routes. From observation it seems that the Dudh Kosi Valley may be a major flyway for migrating birds in the Sagarmatha region. The Dark Kite, a species which is easily recognised by the rapid beating of its wings and its hovering flight, is often seen heading up this valley, while Brown-headed and Black-headed Gulls have been seen on Gokyo Lake, where they rest before departing up-valley towards Cho Oyo.

Wings outspread and motionless, the Himalayan Griffon circles the sky on air currents rising from valleys below, searching for carcases on which to scavenge.

Oblivious to the cold water, a pair of Brahmini ducks rests on Gokyo Lake during their migration northward to Tibet, where they will spend the summer.

Sherpas also speak of *Karangkurung* (Demoiselle Cranes) coming down the Dudh Kosi in the autumn when they overfly Khumbjung and Namche, honking and calling as they head south. Cranes are not seen on the spring migration.

Other migratory birds in the Dudh Kosi include ducks, although their numbers on the Gokyo Lakes remains small, and it is possible that the majority of waterbirds touch down because they are sick or storm driven. The same species of ducks and geese are seen repeatedly on these lakes. Of approximately fifteen species of waterfowl that most likely migrate over Nepal, only six species are known from the Sagarmatha region. The most common Khumbu ducks and geese are the Tufted Pochard, Brahminy Duck, Eurasian Wigeon, Gadwall, Common Pochard, Pintail and Barheaded Goose.

Beyond the yellow cliffs above Sarnasa, the trail drops down to Phunki Tenga where a fine birch forest covers the slopes opposite the tea houses. These trees with their associated catkins, insects and shelter provide a habitat suitable for many small birds. Here, among the trees, peering into crevices of the bark, or beneath the serrate-edged leaves, three species of Tits, the Coal, Sikkim Black, and Crested Brown may be found as well as the Northern Tree Creeper and Orange-barred Leaf Warbler.

At ground level in birch forests other small birds such as the Orange-flanked Bush Robin and the shy White-browed Robin are often found. Both species feed primarily on the ground and flit to low branches to sleep and rest.

Birch forest is also the habitat of Blood Pheasants. The males feature greenish underparts with red on the tail, breast and face; females come in a warm brown shade with either red or black-tipped bills. Since pheasants, as well as all other species in the Park are protected, they remain tame and can often be approached to within a few metres. They are easily followed as they work through the mossy understorey of the birch forest, picking at the green grass, moss and buds in much the same manner as domestic chickens. The forests from Phunki Tenga to beyond Tengboche Monastery and across from Pangboche are all ideal country for Blood Pheasants.

Few avian sounds ring through the Park at night, but from the birch forest a double 'hoo hoo', the second 'hoo' pitched lower than the first, is sometimes heard. This is the call of the Tawny Wood Owl, a medium-sized mouse and vole catcher. The Owl calls most frequently at dusk and again as a prelude to the dawn.

Above Pangboche on the Everest trail, the tree line is left behind and bird life becomes much reduced in both the number of species and the number of individuals. Some species however are still conspicuous, one being the numerous members of the Crow family (Corvidae). The commonest of these, and one that has about the greatest altitude range of any bird in Nepal, is the Jungle Crow. This ubiquitous camp scavenger seems to know exactly where people picnic and shows up soon after humans arrive. They also feed on leaf and flower buds as well as catching and killing young birds or adults that are infirm. This omnivorous diet allows them more habitat range.

Eye-catching red stripes on the male have earned the Blood Pheasant its name. In contrast, the dusky brown colour of the female provides camouflage when she incubates their eggs in a nest set between boulders on the forest floor.

Noisy, cheeky and prolific, the scavenging Jungle Crow is never far from humans. It ranges over a wide altitude, killing the young, or infirm adults of other birds and animals, as well as feeding on vegetation, or scraps left by humans or other predators.

The Jungle Crow with its rather long wedge-shaped tail and its soaring behaviour, may be mistaken for the Tibetan Raven, but the latter is a much larger bird with a very deep voice. Ravens are not common in the Park although they sometimes congregate around the food packets of mountain-climbing parties. As only one raven nest is currently known in the Park, near Khumbjung, it is thought that most Sagarmatha ravens come over from nesting sites in Tibet.

The Red-billed and Yellow-billed Choughs take first prize as the Park's avian acrobats, playfully sweeping about on brisk air currents. The Red-billed species generally lives at a lower altitude than the Yellow-billed but their ranges overlap to a certain extent. It is only the Yellow-billed that has been seen high on Sagarmatha, following the climbing parties to 8600 metres. The Red-billed Chough feeds by probing into the ground and moss for vegetable matter, while the Yellow-billed takes its food mainly from the surface, finding insects and other items, but depending largely on juniper berries. Large flocks of choughs appear to flow from bush to bush in noisy black waves as they search for berries.

Another noisy occupant of the Park, frequently seen between Pangboche and Gorak Shep, is the Tibetan Snow Cock, which utters its gobble-like call from rock strewn slopes above the tree line. This grey bird, often mistaken for a partridge, is the size of an Impeyan Pheasant (weighing about 2.3 kilograms) but in contrast to the latter, the Snow Cock's cryptic plumage allows it to blend well with surrounding lichen-covered rocks. A side view of the bird shows bold black lines sweeping the flanks, as if an after thought of swift black brush strokes had been used to liven up a rather dull background. The Tibetan Snowcock weighs in as Sagarmatha's largest terrestial bird above 4880 metres.

The splendid Grandala, the male a shining cobalt blue when seen in the sun, also resides above the treeline for much of the year. Aerial flocks of grandalas wheel to elevations of about 5185 metres in summer, but by October they are concentrated at about 4270 metres. As the season cools they continue downhill, so that by mid-winter they may descend to the treeline, and in spring the late snows may force them even lower. Flocks of these beautiful high altitude birds have been seen in May around Lukla at 2800 metres, with some birds feeding on the runway.

Grandalas, classed as thrushes, are extremely agile on the wing, catching insects in the same manner as swallows. They also feed on the ground, constantly moving from one grassy knoll to another, the flock widespread yet still cohesive. The birds appear to remain in flocks all year, with winter assemblages sometimes of over one hundred birds formed by October. They are quite at home in cold weather and take well to blowing snow. They also show considerable poise when landing on sheets of ice such as those at the edge of Gokyo Lake, where they skid along the slippery surface without losing their composure or falling over.

Accentors are another very high altitude family best seen at the heads of the Park valleys in places such as Gokyo, Pheriche, Lobuche, Chukong and above Thami. This family of only twelve species appears most highly developed in Central Asia. Five species occur in the Park. Although they resemble sparrows in size and colouration, they retain rather thin bills and behave in a similar manner to thrushes. Their food consists of insects and seeds, and they have a gizzard containing grit to grind the latter. The Alpine Accentor, a species that ranges from the European Alps to the Himalaya and Japan, is perhaps the most trusting bird in the Park. Feeding birds will wander to within twentyfive centimetres of humans if they sit still enough. Other accentors, especially the Robin and Rufous-breasted, also perch tamely on the stone walls or hedges lining the Sherpa summer yak encampments.

Some birds occur in upland meadows only in the summer. Among these is the Rose-breasted Pipit, a drab brownish bird with a faint pinkish tinge on the breast when in breeding plumage. During the summer these pipits are possibly the most conspicuous birds from around 4575 metres up to the limits of the grass. In winter they spread over lowland Nepal and wander into the Indian plains, usually staying close to damp regions bordering lakes and streams. Their association with damp regions carries over throughout the seasons, for in summer when monsoon rains soak everything, the pipits are in their element.

While many species of birds in the Park wander up and down, depending on the season, a hardy few remain at high elevations throughout the entire year. An altitude of up to 4575 metres must be reached before the Red-breasted Rose Finch, Brandt's Mountain Finch and the Horned Lark, birds in this category, become obvious.

As well as resident birds, migrants and summer nesters, there are also the winter visitors. These comprise only a small portion of the Park's birds, because most of the species that winter in Nepal pass over the high country to spend the season in the lower reaches. The White-throated Redstart, though, is an exception and this conspicuous bird is often seen perched on upright posts and hedge tops from about 3050 to 3660 metres during the winter months of early October to early April. Only rarely does the White-throated Redstart stray below 3050 metres and so may be listed as one of the Park's winter visitors.

Another winter visitor is the Black-throated Thrush, a bird of forest edges and orchards, which arrives here in October and November, stays until late April, then returns to its Siberian nesting grounds. In contrast to the White-throated Redstart, the Black-throated Thrush spreads out over a wide altitude band during the winter, from 1220 metres in midland Nepal up to about 3660 metres in the Park. A curious colour dimorphism occurs in this thrush with black-throated and red-throated forms. The red-throated variety breeds in eastern North Asia and winters largely to the north of the Himalaya, and as a result is only occasionally seen in the Park, while the black-throated sub-species predominates.

Understanding of the migratory movements, the general behaviour patterns of the Sagarmatha birds, or even their presence or absence is just in its infancy. But with increased access to the Park allowing additional observers to record data, it is expected that in time the birds of the region will become among the best known in the entire Himalayan chain.

An insect hunter of high alpine meadows, the Robin Accentor is probably one of the tamest birds in Sagarmatha. In winter when insects are scarce it feeds on seeds, and will often wander close to humans as it searches for food.

(Opposite): Often heard but not seen, the noisy Tibetan Snowcock blends well with its rocky surroundings above the tree line. Weighing over two kilograms, this large partridge-like bird indicates its presence with a gobbling call.

Summer in the Himalaya is a time for flowers and insects and an Indian Tortoiseshell butterfly, a bee and a fly all take sustenance provided by the flowers of a ragwort.

Butterflies

Nepal is renowned for its many different species of butterflies, found there because of the wide range of altitudes within its borders. They vary from vivid tropical species, the size of small birds, to tiny inconspicuous high altitude dwellers.

Within the boundaries of Sagarmatha National Park only twentysix species are found. Like most butterflies they are summer creatures only, generally not seen by the majority of visitors, although a few appear in spring and stragglers can still be found in late November.

Like other creatures they occupy differing habitats: streamsides, windy ridges, damp areas, forests, and rocky hillsides. The general impression is that they are sun lovers and to a certain extent this is true. Even during the summer months they are only out and about while the sun is shining, disappearing once the clouds and mist have rolled in. There are some species, however, that prefer the dark shade of wooded areas and do not mind that the sun has been veiled over.

One of the first to appear each summer is the Common Yellow Swallowtail. This attractive butterfly, with its black and yellow markings and obvious tails, is one of the largest in the Park and may be found in abundance from mid-May to June, up to 5000 metres. It shows a preference for open, often very exposed country and seems to delight in being buffeted by the wind on ridges and hilltops. By contrast, it is also often found congregating on the damp ground near rivers and springs.

An even earlier appearance is made by the Snow Apollos (Genus Parnassius). These are scarcely recognisable as belonging to the same family as the swallowtails, for they have no tails to their hindwings and are small and fluttery. Their wings are often semi-transparent, but they can travel surprisingly fast up and down steep hillsides, and like the Common Yellow Swallowtail they can fly in very strong winds. Another distinguishing feature is their habit of settling on the ground with their wings spread out. The Common Blue Apollo flies throughout the summer and is frequently found in the Park. Its markings vary considerably. The dry season form which appears from April to June is white and very lightly spotted, and has been recorded from 3800 to 4800 metres. The wet season form found from July to September is heavily suffused with black scales, giving it a grey colour. The latter flies at slightly lower altitudes, from 3500 to 4400 metres, a tendency to descend in altitude at the end of the season that is shared with other species of butterfly.

Other very common butterflies which appear from about April onwards are the Dark Clouded Yellows, Pale Hedge Blues, Indian Tortoiseshell, Painted Ladies and the Queen of Spain Fritillaries. The appropriately named Hedge Blues are small, pale blue butterflies which are usually found around bushes and are the lowest altitude dwellers. The males are plain blue on their upper sides, while the females have pronounced black borders to their wings.

The Dark Clouded Yellow, a smallish species which may be either bright orange or yellow, as the male and female have different forms, can be found up to 5200 metres, flying fast over open country or settling on flowers low in the grass.

Herald of summer, the beautiful Common Yellow Swallowtail is stronger than a delicate appearance would belie, for it likes exposed, windy ridge tops as well as damp ground near rivers and streams.

The Queen of Spain Fritillary is found up to 4800 metres, and the Painted Lady, a familiar European butterfly, occurs up to 5000 metres. Although they are similar in size and shape, the Queen of Spain is easily distinguished by the angular silver spots on its underside. The Painted Lady seems to prefer exposed ridges and hilltops. Its close relative, the Indian Red Admiral, often chooses the same habitats but does not fly to such high altitudes. It has only been recorded up to 3900 metres and is easily distinguished in flight by its darker colour.

The Indian Tortoiseshell is also closely related to the last two species. It is a small butterfly which is very abundant throughout the season, and has been recorded up to 5200 metres. Although it is usually seen chasing around the hilltops, it is also often seen in numbers, sitting calmly on damp patches near streams, and is the only species other than the Common Yellow Swallowtail that does this. The amount of dark scaling on the wings is variable, indicating that the Tortoiseshell either lives for a very long time or becomes damaged very quickly. Specimens have been found with so little wing area left that it is surprising they can still fly.

The familiar Cabbage Whites are also fairly common in the lower parts of the Park throughout the summer, usually on or near cultivated land. The Large Cabbage White has been recorded up to 4200 metres, and the smaller Indian Cabbage White up to 3700 metres.

Two frequently overlooked early-comers are the Nepal Skipper and the Orange and Silver Mountain Hopper. These tiny butterflies appear from early March to June. The Nepal Skipper is common in open country up to 4400 metres. It is black-and-white-chequered and has a rapid, darting flight which is difficult to follow,although it often settles on bushes or grass.

In contrast, the Orange and Silver Mountain Hopper is relatively uncommon. Slightly smaller than the Nepal Skipper, the Orange and Silver Mountain Hopper has the white replaced by orange and silver markings on the underside, and its flight is much weaker. It is often disturbed as it sits in the middle of paths, between 3600 and 3750 metres.

In early June the first of the Satyrs appears. These large, impressive butterflies with velvety black wings banded in white, show up vividly when settled on plants or flowers, which they love, but they are remarkably well camouflaged on rough rock surfaces. There are three species — the Great Satyr, the Common, and the Narrow Banded Satyrs, the main difference being their size. The Great Satyr is the largest of the three species and is also the first to appear in the summer, in lightly wooded country. The other two are much smaller and do not appear until later in the season when they are common in more open country, between 3000 and 4000 metres.

The Pamir Clouded Yellow, which belongs to the same genus as the Dark Clouded Yellow, also appears in June. Its wings are grey above and a yellow/green colour below. In flight this butterfly looks like a very small Snow Apollo. Although it is generally rare in Nepal, it is not uncommon in the higher areas of the Park and has been recorded from 3400 to 4950 metres, the lower altitudes being later in the season.

Another rare butterfly which tends to fly at higher altitudes is the Common Red Apollo. It is similar to the Blue Apollo but is smaller, with red spotted wings, having been recorded in July and August from 4400 metres up to the snow line at 5300 metres.

Several other species which are fairly common in the Park only appear during July and August. The Peablue, a migrant butterfly found in the lower regions of Nepal in early spring, makes its appearance in the Park during mid summer, and has been recorded up to 3800 metres. It is very

White-banded, velvety black wings help to camouflage the Satyr when it alights on rocks, but not when it is feeding on flowers. The Great Satyr shown here is the largest of three species of Satyrs which appear in the Park during summer.

Opening and closing its wings as it rests, a Queen of Spain Fritillary displays the orange and black spotted upper wing surface which contrasts with angular silver markings on the under surface.

similar to the Hedge Blue but is distinguishable by the hairlike tails on its hindwings. The Common Brimstone, a large vivid yellow butterfly which also prefers the lower regions of the Park up to 3600 metres, is only found during the height of summer, as is the Large Silverstripe, a magnificent creature occasionally found on flowers in woodland clearings up to the same altitude. This large butterfly, which is orange and black above and green and silver striped below is unmistakeable.

All the butterflies mentioned so far are sun lovers, but there is a group which prefers forests and shady places. These are the Browns and several species are found in the Park later in summer. They are more common around the lower border areas but a few are found up to 4000 metres. There are three species of Woodbrowns; the Common Woodbrown, Small Woodbrown and Barred Woodbrown. They are all smallish butterflies which are brown or almost black above, with a clear series of marginal rings below. They prefer low shady places and will visit damp soil and flowers.

The Forks, which are of the same genus but much more interesting than the Woodbrowns in regard to wing shape and pattern, tend to fly higher around trees, but also visit flowers and are occasionally found on paths. The Small Silverfork is quite common up to 4100 metres in July and August, but the Small Golden Fork seems rare by comparison.

A brighter relative which is comparatively scarce in July, but plentiful in August, is the Small Tawny Wall. It often settles on flowers or bushes with its wings open, which is unusual for Browns, showing the very attractive upperside pattern of orange and black. Its upper limit is about 3400 metres.

Occasionally upper Midland butterflies may wander or be blown to altitudes to which they would not normally fly. A few have been recorded in the Park far above their normal altitudinal range, but these are not considered to be true inhabitants of the area.

Trapped by sticky droplets on the leaves of a sundew, a brilliantly hued moth awaits a slow death.

Trader and buyer crowd together in a mixture of ethnic groups at Namche Bazar's Saturday market. Tamang and Rai porters from more fertile, lower regions of Nepal bring foodstuffs which the Sherpas and Tibetans of Khumbu will pay cash for, earned from western and Japanese tourists.

Origins

The name Sherpa, coming from the words *shar* meaning east and *pa*, people, supports the earliest writings which indicate that they originated in the province of Kham in eastern Tibet, some 1250 kilometres from their present homeland. Little is known of Sherpa history but it is believed that they left Kham during the late 1400s or early 1500s because of political and military pressures from the neighbouring Chinese or Mongols, or for religious reasons. They paused briefly in the southern-central Tibetan area before crossing the high Himalayan passes, including the Nangpa La, to reach the Solu Khumbu. The Khumbu was one of four *beyul*, sacred and hidden valleys of refuge created by the Guru Rimpoche, the founder of their religious sect.

This small group was the first wave of migration and was to create the unique Sherpa clan system. At least one of these first clans left the Khumbu to settle in the Solu region while newer clans are said to have arrived in two waves between 1750 and 1850.

It appears that during the 1800s the Sherpa economy was revitalised. This is attributed to the accidental crossbreeding of the yak and cow and the introduction of the British potato into the Sherpa agricultural system. The cross-breed, called the *zopkiok*, provided an animal that produced more milk, lived far longer, tolerated lower altitudes and became a new source of trade with Tibet. The potato is thought to have come from the colonial gardens of Darjeeling, or even perhaps from the 1774 East India Company expedition to Lhasa where the envoy was instructed to plant potatoes at each resting place. These resulted in a significant increase in the Sherpa population; new temples were constructed and by the early 1900s monasteries were being built.

At that time the Sherpas were numerous in the Darjeeling area where they were being employed by British colonial explorers. More travelled to Darjeeling during the 1920s seeking work in the tea plantations, and because of their personal qualities many were employed by the first European expeditions for the Tibetan-based mountain ascents.

The highlanders of Khumbu stand out as a people distinctive in their character, their civic sense and their mode of adaptation to life in extreme altitudes.

Christopher von Furer-Haimendorf, in "The Sherpas of Nepal" Oxford University Press, 1964.

1950 saw the first expedition to Everest from within Nepal's borders, and with it came the beginning of a western influence that was to greatly affect Sherpa living standards. Schools, hospitals, health posts, postal services, air transport and wireless communications came and were absorbed into their way of life; and their semi-nomadic life as herdsmen and traders changed in emphasis with the growth of tourism and trekking.

For centuries the Sherpas have travelled the glaciers of Khumbu, and crossed the high passes between Nepal and Tibet during trading expeditions, using their sure-footed yaks which are both beast of burden and supplier of food and wool. They still travel throughout the Park in the same manner, but today the supplies they bring are for expeditions and trekkers.

Sacred and inviolable, Khumbu-yul-lha
mountain is the home of the God of Khumbu.

The Clan

The Sherpa word for clan is *rhu* which means bone. Like bones of the body, the *rhu* is the framework of Sherpa social structure; to be a member of one of the clans is to be a Sherpa. Although 21 clans are named by the Sherpas, some are sub-clans under separate names and a few have possibly become extinct, so the number of true Sherpa clans is given as twelve with four clans predominating. In Solu, most villages contain single clans with all the Sherpa residents of the village belonging to the same clan, while in Khumbu most villages have members from several or many clans.

Because Sherpas believe that the mother gives the blood *(tahk)* to the child and the father the bone *(rhuwak)*, clan membership is passed down through the male members, sons and daughters inheriting the clan of their father until the daughter marries into the clan of her husband. The clan bond is such that they will often refer to a fellow clan member as being "my brother". Within the marriage system, the clan plays a most important role in not permitting sexual relationships between clan members, this being regarded as incestuous, and so all Sherpas marry outside their clan. It also helps in unifying the communities, for clan members gather together several times a year to worship their particular god. Each clan has a mountain or area as its protective deity, and among the many in Sagarmatha National Park are the lake area of Gokyo and the mountains of Tawoche and Lhotse.

Abodes of the clan gods. Each Sherpa clan has
a particular mountain or area as its protective
deity; the Gokyo Lake area and Tawoche Peak
are some.

Foundation of Society — The Family

The foundation of Sherpa society is the family consisting of husband, wife and their unmarried children, who form an independant household, yet are family, clan and community conscious.

The traditonal marriage is arranged by the parents, but should either partner be unwilling, then their wishes are generally respected. Courtship and marriage can be a lengthy process involving three separate ceremonies over a period of several years, giving the couple time to reconsider or establish their own household.

The first of the ceremonies is the betrothal or *sodene* and can be arranged when the couple are still adolescents, or later after becoming lovers. The *dem-chang*, meaning "the beer of tying", is the second of the ceremonies; although the couple will now have a semi-marital relationship, the bride continues to live in her family home while the husband remains in his. The children born after this ceremony are considered legitimate and a payment must be made if the bond is broken. The final stage of the marriage is called *nama titup* or *gyen-kutop* when the husband takes his wife to their own home. She takes with her a dowry which may be cattle, jewellery, clothing, land or household utensils, and the groom's parents give a share of their property, usually a house. It is customary for the youngest son to eventually inherit the family home after caring for his parents and grandparents in their old age.

The Sherpas' traditional polygamous (two women married to one man) and the mostly Tibetan favoured polyandrous (two or three brothers married to one woman) marriages, although once common, were losing

Dressed in their finery, members of a wedding group approach Namche Bazar. This group has walked for four days, bringing the bride from her family home in Solu to her husband's house where she will now live.

No need for clothes or a charcoal brazier in summer when temperatures are warm enough to do without. Sherpa children are content without toys, and household utensils often become playthings.

popularity before being made illegal in Nepal. These marriages were normally undertaken to prevent the division of family property into uneconomic units, or if the marriage proved childless and neither partner wanted a divorce.

The running of the household is a combined effort with all work being considered of equal value. Sherpas and Sherpanis often share the same work. In households where the husband is often absent for long periods of the year, the wife may make completely independent financial decisions as she cares for the family and house.

A birth is a joyful event although pregnancy is not widely mentioned and the actual birth is not publicly acknowledged for several days, within which the name-giving ceremony is performed. Many Sherpas are named after the day of the week that they are born on, these being: Nima (Sunday), Dawa (Monday), Mingma (Tuesday), Lhakpa (Wednesday), Phurba (Thursday), Passang (Friday), and Pemba (Saturday). Between parents and children there is a relationship of warmth and informality creating secure and happy children.

In this region where life is not taken for granted, death is followed by cremation at one of four sites outside the village, with lengthy and complicated religious rites to assist the soul in its fortynine day passage to the place of Boundless Light. The cremation site depends on the deceased's horoscope. The consequences of death reach beyond the great emotional and economic loss to the household, because the Khumbu communities now possess many widows and a larger number of unmarried women than unmarried men. This is partly due to mountaineering fatalities in recent decades.

Always an important member of the family, a grandmother plays with her grandchildren. She will often run the household and mind smaller members of the family while their parents are busy with work away from home.

105

Sherpa Society

Although a Sherpa village is made up of separate households living and functioning independently of one another, it is a well structured community of families, many related by ties of clan kinship, following a social order created by their forebears. At formal gatherings the hierarchy is often quite obvious, with each person seated according to their acknowledged position in the community.

Traditionally, the controlling force of Sherpa society came from their individual wish to avoid humiliating, shameful acts, but there were individuals and groups who policed the village and enforced rules. Fines and retributions were agreed upon for situations like divorce, adultery, illegitimacy and the breaking of agricultural and forestry rules. Violence and murder were and still are considered highly sinful, but the Sherpas did not take it upon themselves to judge or punish, believing that a person will receive just punishment for evil deeds in his next reincarnation. In situations such as these the offender would usually choose to leave the area, thus solving any potential problems.

Within the last twenty years, the government of Nepal has introduced political and economic reform and is working towards unifying the country into a common political system with a national consciousness. It has created the Panchayat, or district council, a system of single party democracy that interconnects all levels of society from the village to the King. This system with its village, district and zone panchayats, elects officials at each level. Land reforms have been introduced to limit large holdings, and a nationwide network of schools and district courts has been set up. This is having a noticeable impact on Sherpa society.

Village affairs lie with a group of villagers elected for a two to three year term. One of these, the *Pradan Panch,* may be the village representative to the district council, the political body that ties the local region into the national system. Two men are elected as *Osho-nawa* to control the use of the village agricultural land and cattle-breeding, with their main duties being the co-ordination of agricultural activities and the prevention of damage to crops. Another man is appointed as the *Shingi-nawa,* the word *shing* being the Sherpa word for wood; he is the guardian of the forests and deals with the community's wood and timber demands and resources. Two further officials are the *Chorumba* and *Chorpen* who are the guardians of the village temple and are responsible for its upkeep and administration. They also maintain law and order during religious celebrations.

The traditional Sherpa system of order is presently adapting and merging with the national system of law courts and government control, with both systems working side by side.

Konjo Chumbi of Khumbjung, an important elder, looks over the fields and houses of his village. This respected man has held the position of *Pradhan Panch* (equivalent to a mayor) and still takes an active role in village affairs.

The Village and its Houses

A survey in 1979 of Sagarmatha National Park gave a count of about 3500 for the Sherpa population, with the largest concentration of 860 living in the adjoining villages of Khumbjung and Khunde. The valley of the Bhote Kosi had a population of approximately 700, while Namche Bazar then held around 500, and the villages beyond, Pangboche and Phortse, having under 300 each. Jorsale, Dingboche, Tengboche, Devoche, Milingo and Pheriche all contained less than 40. The Sherpa population fluctuates according to the seasons. During the monsoon between June and September, it is at its greatest because of the return of those working in tourism and trade. Around June — July, there is a movement from the main

villages to the small summer settlements, the *yersa* in the high pasturelands where livestock are grazed and hay is made. When the livestock return to the main villages in September, the Khumbu population decreases as the men folk return to their trekking and mountaineering jobs.

As well as Sherpa dwellings the main villages have a pale ochre-red painted temple called a *gompa*, an entrance gate, and a rock monument called a *chorten*. There are no buildings for purely public use. The land around the *gompa* is owned by it and is sacred. Trees growing here are protected. The houses usually stand alone or in small groups, except at Namche Bazar where they are sited close together on terraces excavated out of the hillside.

Protected by their proximity to the village gompa, Upper Pangboche Village still has large, mature juniper trees. In fields surrounding the houses are ripe crops of buckwheat and potatoes which will soon be harvested.

Commercial centre of the Khumbu, Namche Bazar is a thriving business community. Across the gorge of the Bhote Kosi River, Mt. Kongde looks down on houses built into the terraced hillside.

Clinging to steep slopes, the traditional style houses
around Thami *Gompa*, which are occupied by its monks,
blend unobtrusively with the mountainside.

The traditional house or *khangba* is constructed to one of three basic
designs, all based on a rectangular shape. The first of these is a single
rectangular block and the other two are variations, with either another
block being added to the existing one to make a very long rectangular
building, or the second block being placed at a 90 degree angle, making an
L-shape. Most homes are two-storeyed with a ridged roof and the ground
floor built partly into the slope.

It is usual for houses to be constructed with the doors and windows
facing south-east, to get the maximum sunshine, very few houses having
doors or windows at the rear of the building. The carved and painted
wooden window frames, are a feature of Sherpa architecture.

The walls are built of rock, without mortar, the outer surface being
covered with clay and whitewash to seal it. The roof is supported by thick
wooden beams which rest on the end walls and run the length of the
building. These are braced from inside by pillars and supports which are
often elaborately carved.

Newer houses at Namche are still built in the traditional rectangle shape, but are larger and often have shops on the ground floors. The older house (lower centre) has had a new wing added to it, with the improvement of glass in its windows.

Brightly painted window frames add colour to the whitewashed houses. Traditional windows did not have glass panes, but were covered with parchment and opened to allow light in and smoke out. Nowadays, with glass becoming available, windows are bigger and the frames often painted instead of being carved. Outside each house a tall pole carries a flag printed with prayers and the Buddhist moral code.

The ground floor of a Sherpa house has one or two rooms which are used as a byre for livestock in winter, and a storage area for fodder, firewood and farm equipment. In the far corner of this floor is a small area set aside for the *Lhu*, the spirit of the land.

Wooden steps lead to the upper floor and the large living room which is the centre of family life as well as being used for sleeping, entertaining and business transactions. The focal point is the household fire, used for cooking meals and limited heating of the house. Because it is a sacred part of the house, food and household scraps are not burnt in the fire for fear of offending the *Lhu*. Chimneys are a recent introduction, but it is more usual for smoke to filter out through the ceilings and windows, preserving the timber and giving the interior its dark tones.

To one side of the hearth is a long bench. The position closest to the fire is occupied by the houseowner and next to it is the seat of honour. The opposite wall contains wide shelves on which large bronze and copper water urns, other metal and wooden containers, and household utensils are placed. These create a subdued glow of gold tones against the darkened woodwork, and reflect the wealth of the family.

Wealthier families have a separate room leading off the living room, the *lhang*, or private temple, which is used for worship. Vividly coloured religious paintings may panel the walls and ceilings, and an altar facing the window holds sacred books and religious vessels. In less wealthy homes, shelves at a corner of the main room serve the same purpose.

At the opposite end of this floor the entrance passage-way can lead to a partly roofed terrace that is often used for the drying of crops for winter storage. If the lavatory, the *chhakhang*, is included in the house, it is sited in a shed on this terrace, and the area beneath is used for the collection of manure.

The small dwellings which many families have in the summer settlements, above the main villages, also serve as storage places for hay until it is carried back for use during the winter.

Old and new ways of life combine. Chinese bowls, brass and modern enamel plates line shelves in a traditional house. The wooden prayer wheel has been covered with plastic to keep it clean.

Sacred and respected, the household fire is the focal point of a Sherpa house. There are usually no chimneys and smoke drifts away through open windows or out between ceiling timbers, preserving them and giving the wood a smoke-blackened polish.

Houses in summer settlements, above the main villages, provide shelter while cattle are being grazed on lush growth in the high pastures, then serve as storage places for hay which will be used as stock food during winter.

Skilfully built, the mortarlesss rock walls of houses are over half a metre thick, with a plaster of mud and whitewash to seal the outer surface. Rooves were traditionally covered with long wooden shingles held down by boulders. The ground floor is used for storage and as a byre for animals, while the upper floor is a family living area.

Religion

The village, with its people involved in agriculture, trade, cattle breeding and tourism, is one side of Sherpa life; the other is found within the religion of the Khumbu. Sherpas follow a form of Tibetan Buddhism (often called Lamaism) of the unreformed, oldest sect named the *Nyingmapa* or "Ancient Ones". It is composed largely of Tantric Mahayana Buddhism of northern India with influences from the pre-Buddhist Tibetan religion of Bon and the Chinese Cha'an Buddhism.

Nepal is important in the history of Buddhism by being the birthplace of its founder, the Gautama Buddha. He was born in a grove of trees at Lumbini on the Terai, around the year 543 BC. Buddhism, however, as practised by the Sherpas, goes back to the 7th century AD when it was introduced to the Tibetans who were *Bon-po*, followers of the *Bon* religion. The *Bon* belief featured the worship of ancestors, as well as gods and goddesses of mountains, fields, rocks and waters, and many of their wrathful spirits were incorporated into Tibetan Buddhism. It is found today as part of the Sherpas' religious practice of worshipping clan gods and spirits of the countryside and houses.

In the latter part of the 8th century AD a Tibetan king brought two Indian teachers from Nepal. One of these was Padmasambhava, a teacher, magician and sorcerer whom the Sherpas called Guru Rimpoche. He prepared for the final establishment of Buddhism in Tibet by defeating and subduing demons and hostile local gods and making them into protectors of the faith. The *Nyingmapa* sect claim him as their founder and the mani engravings and chant "Om mani padme hum" are addressed to this leader.

Another figure prominent in the Sherpas' religion is their patron saint, Lama Sangwa Dorje, the founder of the first village temples in the Khumbu. While legend records that he flew to the Khumbu from Tibet, it is also said that he was born at Mo-ng, a place on the trail between Phortse and Khumbjung.

Lama Sangwa Dorje's mystical powers included flying and utilising the rays of the sun and both Tengboche and Pangboche have landmarks that are attributed to his exceptional abilities. The word *teng* means heel and *pang* is hand and at these religious sites are the imprints of his body in rock.

The world of the monasteries is separate from the village life and religion. The monks officiate at some village ceremonies but not those which are strongly related to Bon Buddhism and conducted by the village *Lamas*. The villagers only occasionally attend monastic ceremonies.

The *lama* heading the monastic institutions can have the title *Rimpoche*, meaning "Precious One", indicating that he is the reincarnation of a previous *lama*.

Vivid colours depict a seated Buddha on the walls of a private gompa.

115

The term *lama*, (Tibetan for guru or master), although reserved for heads of monasteries, is mainly used by the Sherpas when referring to the village priest. All the members of the religious communities have the choice of either living in the villages as part of the community, or devoting themselves to an entirely spiritual life in the monasteries and nunneries. The monastic vows for the majority of those that take them signify a lifelong commitment.

Under his guidance are the *thawa*, or monks, who reside in the houses surrounding the monastery. Tengboche and Thami are celibate monasteries but other religious establishments have monks and *lamas* who may be married. There are two nunneries in the Khumbu, one at Devoche, near Tengboche, and the other at Thamo, between Namche Bazar and Thami. In these reside the celibate nuns called *arni*.

The village religion can also include the *lha-wah*, the spirit medium whose main function is to cure illness through a trance-like communication with the spirits. This very old custom originated in early Tibet.

A front row in the audience gives these nuns an uninterrupted view of the Mani Rimdu dances, and while watching they drink traditional salt and butter tea from shallow, lidded bowls. Like the monks, their hair is close cropped and often covered with a pointed bonnet.

The Sherpa Year

The Sherpa years, like the Chinese, are not shown in numbers but in symbols, which are the horse, sheep, monkey, bird, dog, pig, rat, ox, tiger, hare, dragon and snake. Some years are considered by the Sherpas as being good or bad for certain activities. An example of this is the year of the monkey when building and marriages are not undertaken. This unfavourable year is customarily shortened to last only eleven months, with the new year celebrations beginning one month earlier to encourage the year's ending. A woman born in the year of the tiger finds it extremely difficult to find a husband regardless of how beautiful she may be.

Village routine, religious rites and celebrations are calculated by the village *lama* from astrological charts and the Old Buddhist calendar. The dates vary from year to year, with an annual event being unlikely to fall on the same day every year.

The new year begins in January with the yearly house-cleaning. Lucky symbols are painted on house walls and the new year *Losar* festivities take place. It is a time of feasting, singing and dancing that can last for weeks, while the fields lie dormant awaiting the spring.

In March walls are repaired and firewood collected. Mounds of compost are heaped on the thawed fields and then worked into the soil. With the coming of spring in April potatoes, buckwheat and barley are sown. The sheep are shorn and yaks brought to the villages for the cutting and plucking of their hair.

Changing seasons influence a year's activities and Sherpa lives. In early spring manure is cleaned from the ground floors of houses and dumped in mounds on the fields, ready to be dug in as fertiliser before crops are planted (1). With the arrival of summer, cattle are taken to high pastures and their milk made into curd, or dried to form a hard cheese (2). As autumn approaches grass is cut with small scythes and made into hay which will be stored for winter fodder (3). Firewood is collected before winter sets in (4), and fleeces washed ready for spinning and weaving during the long cold months (5). Carrying water is always an arduous task but it is made much harder by snowfalls. Snow is never melted down for water as too much firewood is burned in the process (6). 1

118

The rite of *Chirim* is performed by the village *lama* to drive off the evil spirits, with symbolic dough figures and grain thrown beyond the village boundaries. Officials or *nawa* are selected and the annual *yul-thim* or village meeting takes place, when the rules of the village are agreed upon for the year. This is followed by the *Osho* rite, to protect the lands and newly sown crops, during which the villages are surrounded by a magical boundary and the evil spirits banished beyond.

The flowering of the rhododendrons in May heralds the new life for the year.

Fields are daily becoming greener, calves and lambs are born, and the men return from trekking in time for the *Mani Rimdu* celebrations at Thami. Occasional yak trains, laden with goods, still set off to travel the centuries-old trade route over the Nangpa La to Tibet. The *Niugne* rite is performed in late May or early June to cleanse the worshippers of sin. It is usually practised by the old and pious, and involves meditation, fasting, silence, and the circling of the village *chortens* and *mani* walls.

By June, clouds are rolling up the valley in the early morning and the three-month-long monsoon is beginning. The centuries-old *Dumji* festival, to request the gods' support against evil forces and to commemorate the death of Khumbu's patron saint, *Lama Sangwa Dorje*, gathers all the villagers together at the *gompas*.

During this five day festival the prayer flags surrounding the villages are replaced, and the *lamas* read texts and dress in costumes to perform ritual dances.

Shortly after this event, all livestock are banned from the villages, and with their movement to the summer pastures go a large number of the villagers. The cattle graze on lush summer grass, butter, cheese and curd being produced from their milk.

During early July a colourful and unusual dance is performed at Namche Bazar by the Tibetan community, to celebrate the birth of their spiritual leader the Dalai Lama.

In the summer villages the celebration of *yer-chang* (summer beer) takes place, when the clan mountain gods are worshipped to secure the welfare of the herds. These celebrations last for as many days as there are families involved in the partying group. In the main villages those that remain guard the fields and celebrate "the fat of the pig" or *Phang-ngi*, a time of happiness and humour. The four days of feasting and dancing conclude when, dressed in comedy clothing, the Sherpas visit other households and picnic on the outskirts of the village.

August is the wettest month when the monsoon is at its height and beneath the mist the Khumbu is clothed in greenery. Then, as the rains ease in September, harvesting begins. The crops are cut, hay made, and the men return to Kathmandu for the trekking season. With the lifting of potatoes and the end of the harvesting, symbolic rock barriers are removed from village entrances, and livestock and villagers return from the summer settlements for the October *Chirim* rite to protect the communities.

Summer — a time for festivities.

Celebration of a spiritual leader's birthday. The Tibetan community picnics while watching costumed actors perform a colourful and humorous dance drama in honour of the Dalai Lama.

Yerchang, or 'summer beer', is a time for blessing animals and crops to ensure their wellbeing and productivity. A beribboned yak has prayers said over her so that she will produce more milk and calves.

Dumji commemorates the death of Khumbu's patron saint, Lama Sangwa Dorje, and requests continued support against evil from the gods. Prayer flags beneath Khumbi-yul-lha rock, on the hillside above Namche Bazar, are replaced each year during this festival.

121

On the full moon of October-November, the ritual *Mani Rimdu* dance takes place again, this time at Tengboche. It is performed to enhance the well-being of the Sherpa people by exorcising demons and evil spirits from the monastery. In richly coloured costumes and masks representing the deities, the monks dance in the spectator-packed courtyard. During the course of the three day event, a procession of *lamas* and monks playing their musical instruments, winds its way down from the monastery to a dais, where offerings are made and blessings given to the Sherpas.

Preparation for winter begins in November when fuel and leaf litter are collected before the arrival of the first snow. It is also a time for the devout to travel on religious pilgrimages to Kathmandu and India; while those remaining spin, weave and hand-feed the livestock.

Winter has come by January, spinning and weaving continue, and houses are repaired. The fields are bare, high winds howl around the peaks and for a few weeks the rains and snowfalls are frequent. The Sherpas prepare for the new year ahead.

Mani Rimdu, an important religious ritual dance, is celebrated at Thami and Tengboche monasteries in May and October/November each year. Before an altar holding symbolic food offerings, the monks, wearing masks and costumes representing dieties and demons, perform thirteen dances in a day-long drama enacting the battle between good and evil.

Monuments and Symbols

The religious architecture in Khumbu is fairly recent despite the Sherpas having settled in the region some 450-500 years ago. It is said that the earliest of these was a small *gompa* at Pangboche built some 300 years ago.

All the monasteries date from this century, the most architecturally important being Tengboche which was originally built around 1915. Destroyed by an earthquake in 1933 it was rebuilt shortly afterwards, almost to the same design.

These light ochre-red coloured monasteries and temples resemble those of Tibet in shape and dimensions. Mostly two and sometimes three-storeyed, with the ground plan in keeping with the sacred mandala design, they are a series of squares rather than the rectangular shape of Sherpa houses.

The entrance to a monastery and temple is through an enclosed, stone-paved forecourt or *cham-ra*, which is ritually circled before entering the main hall or *lha-khang*. The centre point of the hall is the shrine of the principal deity to which the *lha-khang* is dedicated. *Thang-ka* or painted scrolls hang from the ceiling and silk banners are attached to pillar tops. At the entrance there are usually stairs leading up to the floor above the main hall. At Tengboche, the room above the hall contains the library. Above that is the printing room.

Set in a throne room for the gods, Tengboche Gompa is the most important centre of Buddhism in the Park. The thoughts of all who visit here must be influenced by the grandeur of surrounding mountains.

(opposite): Symbolic embodiment of the forces which shape life, a chorten represents earth, water, fire, wind and sun, and the Thirteen Steps to Enlightenment. Within it are prayer books and religious relics. Like all other religious monuments of Khumbu, it is always passed on the left side.

125

Constant reminders of Buddhism are the inscriptions carved or painted on rocks, stones and prayer wheels throughout the Solu-Kumbu. These bear the Tibetan words *"Om mani padme hum"* or "Hail to the jewel of the lotus", a prayer to the founder and spiritual leader, the *Guru Rimpoche*, who was said to be "born of a lotus flower in the middle of a lake".

The *mani* stones are set in walls or placed around *chortens* and are a mark of devotion, with religious merit or *sonam* being gained by both the person who had the stones carved and those that pass by. The *mani* walls, *chortens* and prayer wheels are passed or turned in a clockwise direction, indicating that one is a follower of Buddhism rather than the ancient Bon belief. Likewise, the swastika, an ancient symbol which signifies good luck, branches clockwise in Buddhism and the opposite direction in Bon.

Prayer wheels vary in size from small hand-held ones to some which are several metres in height. The large cylinders are housed in their own buildings, often over streams with the force of the water being used to turn them. The inside of the prayer wheel is packed with printed prayers, the merit gained from the action of the turning wheel offsetting wicked thoughts and deeds.

Found throughout Buddhist Asia is the *chorten*. Known as *stupa* in Nepalese, they are a religious monument dating back to the beginnings of Buddhism. The name *chorten* in Tibetan means a receptacle of offering, and within the *chorten* are prayer books and religious relics. Most *chortens* in Khumbu are based on the Indo/Nepalese design. Those at Tengboche are exceptions because their three designs have their origins in Tibet. The *chorten* incorporates abstract Buddhist concepts making them visible. Sections of the chorten have symbolic meanings: the square base is the earth, the dome being water, the triangular-shaped finial is both fire and the 13 steps to Enlightenment, and the spire or half-moon symbol on the top is the wind and sun. At the entrance to some villages and monasteries are free-standing gateways called *kani*. The geometric mandala design and the deities of Buddhism are painted on the underside of the lintels to keep bad spirits from those that pass through these gateways.

Fabric flags, printed with the *mani* prayers, are found throughout Khumbu on roof tops and in prominent positions around the countryside. Like the *chorten*, the colours represent the natural elements: blue for sky, white for clouds, red for rocks, yellow for earth and green for water. These flags are replaced yearly during the *Dumji* festival; meanwhile the winds, rain and sun combine to carry the prayers to the four corners of the world and beyond. There are numerous mountain gods, the most important of which are Khumbi-yul-lha (Khumbu God), the rocky peak standing above the villages of Khumbjung and Khunde, and Chomolungma, otherwise known as Sagarmatha or Mt Everest. Other sacred mountains include Pumori, (Daughter Mountain), Kangtaiga and Tamserku. Besides these there are many mountains and areas worshipped by the clans. Also of significance to the Sherpas are particular rocks, trees, streams and springs that are believed to be inhabited by the *Lhu* and *dhu*, the secret spirits originating in the ancient Bon belief.

Repetitious as our footfalls, the timeless chant
'Om mani padme hum' is a constant reminder of
Buddhism. Carved forever on a rock beside the
trail, whoever passes it to the left will gain
religious merit.

Music and Dance

The music of the monasteries has often been described as unearthly. Although the actual sound may be lost in the memory, the chord it strikes within the conciousness of the listener remains, for it comes from the very essence of human sounds. The droning chants of the monks and *lamas*, practising their daily devotions, sometimes combined with the temple orchestra, have been passed down through generations of monastic Buddhism.

The written music of the religion consists of waving lines of varying thicknesses which accompany the text to be chanted. These lines indicate when the voice should rise, swell or fall in relation to the words chanted. The sound of the instruments are shown pictorially with the figure of a drumstick, for example, at the appropriate place.

The orchestra includes a small number of wind and percussion instruments. The players of wind instruments, who normally blow in pairs, are trained to breathe through their noses so that the sound will not be interrupted. The large telescoping horn, elaborately decorated in contrasting metals, can extend for several metres and produces a deep, droning tone. Smaller pairs of metal horns, both straight and curved, are also used in the temples and at dance ceremonies. Another form of horn is made of human thigh bone and is often used in ceremonies involving exorcism, for it is thought to be capable of subduing gods and demons. The wind instruments also include conch shells, and a type of oboe which is the only instrument in the orchestra capable of producing a melody.

Cymbals of several sizes, held vertically and horizontally, are used as part of the orchestra and to indicate the beginning and ending of a service. Small cymbals and handbells are also used by monks in their devotions. There are various kinds of drums. One, inherited from India, takes the form of an hour glass with dangling cords, which when vigorously rotated makes small knobs on the ends of the cords strike the drum surface. Another drum is supported on a pole and is struck by a padded ball on the end of a long curved stick.

The religious ritual dances, as performed by the monks and *lamas* at *Mani Rimdu* and *Dumji* ceremonies, follow centuries old Tibetan monastic traditions. Wearing elaborate, brocade costumes, and masks representing the deities, the dancers enact the defeat of evil, encircling and leaping in a blaze of drama and colour.

Unlike religious dances, the social dances of the Sherpas appear subdued. They are performed in a long row, at the centre of which stands the most honoured Sherpa and Sherpani in the gathering. With arms around their fellow dancers, the line extends out in a semi circle, in order according to their heirarchy, with the men on one side and the women on the other. The dance itself consists of a series of forward foot movements accompanied only by voices and the sounds of stamping and shuffling feet. Bodies sway and occasionally break off into small groups to revolve back to the original line. The rhythm and foot movements change at irregular intervals, making the dance an acquired and practised ability, far more complicated than it first appears.

The music of the Khumbu is not only that of religion and entertainment. It may also be heard in yak bells from a distant hill, a river rushing far below, a flock of birds wheeling above, dogs barking and voices calling. In this land where all sounds carry far and clear, the silence of the country beneath Sagarmatha can be as memorable as the music of the Sherpas.

A droning echo, as drawn and deep as the instrument which produces it, issues from the long telescoping horns played by pairs of monks during religious ceremonies.

Sound effects, rather than a melody, are produced by silver-decorated horns, handbells and small drums used by the monastery orchestra during services and rituals.

Like the bleating of lambs, silver decorated horns add shrill punctuation to an already colourful ceremony.

Art

I was struck once again by the over-rich and intricate Himalayan art which is such a contrast to the straightforward clarity of the Himalayan soul.
Michel Peissel. Zanskar.

The master artist, known to the Sherpas as *kappa,* led a wandering existence travelling from monastery to temple, decorating them in the traditional style with a knowledge and expertise originating in Tibet. His works of art were usually anonymous and often dateless.

The traditional artist is not particularly honoured in Sherpa society, except for his knowledge of the Buddhist scriptures, which usually goes with the practice of his skills. The first Tibetan trained painter in Khumbu was the renowned *Kappa* Kalden who died in 1981. His expertise is carried on by his son and a small number of students. In Khumbu, wall paintings are most commonly seen, but both wall and scroll paintings are found within the monasteries, temples and private houses. Wall paintings appear to go back to the beginnings of Buddhist art. The paint is applied onto a thick plaster, made from earth mixed with finely chopped straw and then smoothed and sized. The scroll painting or *thang-ka,* for which Tibetan art is most widely known, originated in India. It is painted on cloth, framed in silk and easily carried when rolled up.

The paints were produced from earth, mineral and vegetable substances, ground to powder and then mixed with water, glue and chalk, These were applied in a specific order, with some details being done on astrologically favourable days, while delicate work and the application of gold were left to the end. Many of the subjects painted are devotional or sacred pictures to induce good thoughts, or illustrate examples of good deeds and assist in gaining religious merit. They can also be meditational; to show the theology of Buddhism and to imprint on the mind the images of its followers and the deities. Included in the subjects painted are The Precious Master (Guru Rimpoche or Padme-sambhava); the Buddhas, including the All Noble (Kuntubzang-po or Samanthabhadra) and the great saviour The Glancing Eye (Pawa Cherezi or Avalokitesvara).

Widely found in the entrance way to religious buildings and in private temples are paintings of the Guardians of the Four Quarters and the Wheel of Life. This distinctive wheel is held by a demonic figure, with the six compartments of the wheel representing the good and bad worlds into which one may be reborn. Around the rim of the wheel are smaller scenes symbolizing the twelve stages by which reincarnation takes place, and at the centre are three animals representing lust (a cockerel), anger (a snake) and ignorance (a pig), these being the three main obstacles to Enlightenment.

It is only recently that Khumbu artists have begun painting for the tourist market. These few painters now use water colours but their subjects are still traditional, portraying religion or good thoughts, such as the Wheel of Life and Animals of Friendship. The most sought after however, are their stylised landscapes showing the villages and monasteries set amongst the mountains of Sagarmatha National Park.

Gilded Buddhas and richly coloured, intricate designs decorate interior walls of the gompas.

Skills learned in Tibet are applied by the old master painter, Kappa Kalden, as he works on one of his last paintings.

131

Crafts

Few Khumbu Sherpas can be regarded as craftsmen or women, because their traditional lives as traders, farmers and cattle breeders gave them the means to employ specialized and skilled labourers from among other ethnic groups. The Sherpas evaluate a person's work according to its usefulness and the profit gained from it.

Formal education is highly valued while skills are regarded as less important, as they are in most of Nepal. Carpentry is considered a worthy skill and carpenters employed on house building are relatively well paid, although it is seldom a full time occupation. The wooden domestic utensils found in most houses originate from outside Khumbu. Although once imported from Tibet they are now produced in the lower regions of Nepal by other ethnic groups. The stone mason is normally a Sherpa, and this skilled labourer, using crude tools, creates from the rocks of Khumbu the religious carvings and stones for house building.

The *kami,* or blacksmith/metal worker, belonged to one of the lowest castes of Nepalese society. Although not usually caste conscious, the Sherpas followed the Hindus in not admitting blacksmiths to their houses until 1970, when the caste system was abolished in Nepal. Where traditional clothing is concerned, the Sherpa/Tibetan felt and hide boots are made by professional boot-makers, who are usually immigrants from Tibet, while tailors and dressmakers are from other ethnic groups; neither of these crafts being highly esteemed by the Sherpa people.

While it is becoming increasingly common for synthetic products and fabrics to be purchased in Kathmandu, spinning is still an occupation shared by both Sherpa and Sherpani. Men can often be seen walking about the villages with a sheep fleece in their left hand while their right turns the spindle. The weaving of yak hair blankets, aprons and woollen fabric is done by the women on two types of loom. One is a simple loom stretching many metres in length and less than half a metre wide, the other being a treadle loom, reputedly introduced from Tibet as recently as the beginning of this century.

Preparing and spinning a fleece is a family occupation.

Metres of narrow cloth produced on these long looms are cut and joined to make mats, bags, aprons and other clothing.

Suspended by neckbands woven from yak hair, a selection of brass cattle bells hang in the doorway of a Namche shop.

From rough stones the skilled stonemason patiently chips out straight-sided building blocks.

Clothing and Jewellery

It is during religious celebrations and festivities that traditional clothing and jewellery are seen at their finest in contrast to the rather subdued colours normally worn.

The clothing of the Sherpani, although perhaps appearing otherwise, is practical, comfortable and most suitable for their life and environment. Called an *ingi*, it consists of a spacious ankle-length dress, crossing at the front and secured at the waist with a tight sash to create a pocket-like flap above, that serves as a purse. This is traditionally worn over a brightly coloured silk blouse. Striped aprons, a short one in front and a thicker longer one behind, add warmth, colour and practicality to the costume.

The older Sherpas, and the younger men on formal occasions, wear a *chu-pah*. This loose, very long sleeved coat is belted at the waist and worn over a shirt and trousers. It is often draped off one shoulder or left to hang from the belt on warm days.

Although many kinds of hats are worn, including the older style brocade cap with ear flaps and wool lining, the type most commonly seen on formal occasions is the wide brimmed, off-white felt hat which is a relatively recent introduction from India.

The monks, *lamas* and nuns wear several types of outer garments, all dark red in colour, the dye being obtained from the fir cone and fixed with rock salt. These are usually worn over yellow or saffron coloured shirts or tops. The outer garments are sleeveless and often in the same basic design as the *ingi* or *chu-pah*. The clerical men may also wear a skirt which is gathered at the waist by a sash and worn with a waistcoat. Long-sleeved jackets, or shawls which run across the body covering the left shoulder only, are worn in cooler weather.

The jewellery is more than decorative for it can be a symbol of the wealth and status of the household. On special occasions the Sherpanis wear distinctive silver charm boxes and large waist clasps. These can be elaborately worked with scrolling and other designs and set with stones of turquoise and coral. Ear-rings are widely worn by both women and the older men, but the heavily gold-hooped design carrying a turquoise or coral pendant, sometimes seen supported by a thong over the ear, is favoured by Tibetan men. Necklaces, some strands reaching to well below the waist, string together the blue turquoise, *yhew*, red or pink coral, *churuk*, yellow amber, seed pearls and the prized black and off-white striped stone, *szi;* all acquired from centuries of Tibetan trading or nowadays in the market places of Kathmandu and India.

A symbol of household status and wealth, jewellery is usually worn on special occasions only. The Sherpanis' traditional dark-coloured dress, called an *ingi*, is often worn with several layers of coloured blouses and striped aprons for warmth.

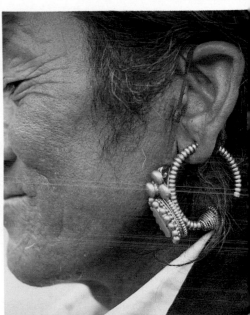

A pensive young Sherpani wears her back apron folded diagonally and held by a silver clasp.

A Tibetan man supports his heavy gold and turquoise ear-ring by a thong over his ear.

The traditional coat, or *chu-pah,* is usually made of cloth, but older men will sometimes wear one made from sheepskin for warmth.

Food and Drink

The Sherpa diet is mainly one of pleasantly bland starch foods accompanied either by side dishes or mildly spiced or hot sauces. Barley and buckwheat appear to have been the crops on which the Sherpas lived until the potato was brought to the Khumbu just over a hundred years ago, to become the basis of their diet. The potato, or *rigi,* is eaten in many forms. It is usually boiled, either alone or as a stew, can be cooked in oil with spices and garlic, or made into a pancake. The traditional barley flour òr *tsampa* is stirred into tea to make a paste-like cereal. Buckwheat flour is cooked into a thick dough-like mixture, small portions of which are pulled off and then dipped in a hot sauce.

Meat and green vegetables, both raw and dried, are used in stews, called *shakpa,* or as side dishes. These are either locally grown or obtained from the bazaar. Rice, lentils and noodles reflect the Nepalese and Chinese influences and are also purchased from the bazaar, as are small quantities of seasonal fruits which include tangerines, apples, peaches, bananas, and the *naspati,* sometimes called the Asian pear.

The protein foods such as yoghurt, curd, butter, and a form of cheese which is dried into small hard pieces, are widely eaten throughout the Khumbu, but eggs are far less popular with Sherpas.

The day to day food gives the impression of being somewhat limited in variety, but this image is dispelled by the delicious and ingeniously created foods offered at special occasions. Within this category come the stuffed pastries, such as the *momo;* a type of sausage containing *tsampa* and spices; and a thick, jelly-like substance, tasting not unlike liver, which is obtained by puncturing the veins of yaks just prior to the breeding season. A specialty in summer is a fungus that is comparable to the mushroom in taste.

Tea, with milk and sugar is the usual drink. The traditional salt and butter tea, called *solchha,* although sipped in private homes, is rarely offered in hotels and tea-houses.

Rice or millet is fermented with a type of yeast to make the very popular *chang* or beer, and further distilling produces the stronger spirit *aarak* or *rakshi* (Nepalese), drunk by many Asian peoples.

Pounding with a heavy stone pestle breaks down grains of rice to produce a coarse flour which cooks quickly.

136

Humble but important, potatoes form the mainstay of a Sherpa's diet.

The *chang* flows freely at special occasions. Made from fermented rice or millet, this milky beer is brought to parties in large brass decorated, wooden containers.

A simple balance weighs onions and butter at the bazaar. Other vegetables are sold by the piece or in bundles, while grains are sold by volume, measured by a brass container.

137

Footsteps Through Time

It seemed to look down with cold indifference on me, mere puny man, and howl derision in wind gusts at my petition to yield up its secret, this mystery of my friends.

N.E. Odell
on the disappearance of Mallory
and Irvine on Everest, 1924.

Without help from oxygen or modern clothing and equipment, Mallory and Norton are shown here climbing at 8224 metres (26,985 feet), in 1922.

Edmund Hillary and Sherpa Tenzing Norgay, the first men to reach the summit of Sagarmatha, in 1953, pause for a rest at 8290 metre (27,200 feet).

Early Visitors

George Leigh Mallory was probably the first foreigner to see the Nepalese side of Sagarmatha and the head of the Khumbu Valley when he looked down from the Lho La, the saddle on the Nepal/Tibet border just above the present Base Camp site, during the first reconnaissance expedition in 1921. But this was just a glimpse because the borders of Nepal were closed to foreigners and Mallory had reached the Lho La from the Tibetan side. Khumbu remained hidden from those early European explorers, botanists and surveyors who were slowly mapping out the rest of the world, and its only visitors were Nepalese botanists.

Major Lal Dhwoj, a retired Army Officer, came in 1930 and made a fairly extensive botanical survey of Khumbu and the adjoining areas of Solu and Rolwaling. Of the 666 specimens he collected, his most exciting find was the dwarf Himalayan Poppy which was named after him, *Meconopsis dhwojii*. It is now found in many private collections and botanic gardens around the world.

Major Dhwoj was followed in 1933 by another Nepali, K.N. Sharma, who continued his work. An Indian, M.L. Banerji, also made five pre-monsoon visits to east Nepal between 1948 and 1955. Presumably he was able to enter Nepal because his nationality was Indian, and not that of a western country. Although Banerji went to Khumbu his routes are uncertain.

Once restrictions on entering Nepal were lifted in the late 1940's, the number of foreign visitors increased dramatically, with expeditions becoming commonplace. Among the first of these visitors were the noted mountaineers Charles Houston, H.W. Tilman and Eric Shipton, and the most well known expedition, the 1951 reconnaissance of Sagarmatha.

Three men who have played a part in the history of Sagarmatha, Sir Edmund Hillary (centre), the first man to reach the top in 1953, with Tenzing Norgay Sherpa, is pictured here with Peter Habeler and Rheinhold Messner after their successful first ascent without oxygen in 1978.

140

The Highest Summit

According to a popular story, an official of the Indian Trigonometrical Survey burst into the office of his superior in New Delhi one day in 1852 and exclaimed,

"Sir, I have discovered the highest mountain in the world".

In fact the discovery was far less dramatic and was only the final product of laborious cross-checking of figures from the field survey. Nepal was closed to Europeans at that time, and for almost a century afterwards the height of its major peaks could be calculated only from the Indian hills, nearly 150 kilometres away. The surveyors were remarkably accurate with their primitive equipment. They found Everest to be 29,002 feet high, and recalculations in 1953-55 gave its height as 29,029 feet. The Chinese have since done further calculations and claim it to be 29,145 feet (8885 metres), but it is generally accepted to be 29,028 feet, (8848 metres).

Before 1852 Everest was unknown to westerners because it was inaccessible, and all but its summit was hidden from the Indian plains by its giant neighbours Lhotse and Nuptse. For several years the newly discovered peak was known by its code number XV in the survey book; it was not until 1865 that it was given the name Everest by Sir Andrew Waugh, Director of the Survey of India. He suggested that it should be named after his distinguished predecessor, Sir George Everest, Surveyor General of India from 1830 to 1843. It is the only mountain in the entire range that bears the name of an individual. The Tibetan name Chomolungma was discovered a short time later, and it has been proposed as more suitable for a mountain that has been venerated under that name for centuries before Sir George Everest's was known. Sagarmatha, meaning 'Mother of the Universe' is the official Nepalese name.

A circuit of Everest, from Darjeeling to Kathmandu, was made by surveyors in 1871; but the northern Tibetan side remained closed to others, as was the southern Nepalese side, until 1920 when the goodwill of the Dalai Lama was secured. The British reconnaissance expedition in 1921, with George Mallory as one of the climbers, inspected the mountain and, although the Western Cwm (Mallory's name) was discovered, it was thought that the Khumbu Icefall would be insurmountable. This route was also in Nepal and out of bounds, so attention was turned to a route from the North Col on the Tibetan side.

The first attempt on the summit was made in 1922 by an expedition led by General C.G. Bruce, with George Mallory, George Finch, Howard Somervell, E.F. Norton, and A.W. Wakefield as climbers. Finch and Bruce reached a height of 27,300 feet (8323 metres) using open circuit oxygen apparatus. This was the highest point then reached by man. The expedition was abandoned when an avalanche claimed the lives of seven Sherpas.

With hopes set high for a successful ascent, some of the 1924 Everest Expedition members pose at their base camp. They are from left, back row: Irvine, Mallory, Norton, Odell, MacDonald. Front row: Shebbeare, Bruce, Somervell and Beetham. Of them Mallory and Irvine never returned.

Another attempt was launched in 1924. Hopes were high this time as men had climbed and camped higher than ever before, and valuable lessons had been learnt as to the importance of adequate food and proper support. The climbers again included Mallory, Norton, and Somervell, with Andrew Irvine and five others. Norton and Somervell were able to establish camp at 26,000 feet (7927 metres), and from it Norton reached a height of 28,126 feet (8575 metres) by traversing up and across the Yellow Rock Band. A few days later, on June 8th, Mallory and Irvine made their ill-fated attempt on the summit. Odell, climbing up from Camp V, saw through a rent in the mist two figures on a snow slope below a rock step on the north-east ridge. They were about 600 metres away and it was 12.30 p.m. From what Odell saw and the position of the ice axe found in 1933, it seems probable that the accident to Mallory and Irvine must have occurred as they were descending, having been defeated by the first or second rock step. Speculation as to their fate has never ceased.

Eight years passed before the Dali Lama would give permission for another Everest attempt. This was in 1933, and on his insistence all members of the expedition were British. Hugh Ruttledge was leader. Wyn Harris and Wager attempted the summit from Camp IV at 27,400 feet (8353 metres) and found Irvine's ice axe about 250 metres from the First Step, which they were able to climb. They were turned back however by the Second Step. Further attempts across the face route taken by Norton in 1924 were more successful than along the ridge, but new snow on the face forced a retreat from the same point reached in that expedition. The onset of the monsoon ended all further attempts that year.

In 1935, a reconnaissance during the monsoon, led by Eric Shipton, established that climbing conditions above 23,000 feet (7012 metres) were unsuitable at that time of the year. The following year another expedition, led by Ruttledge again, was defeated by the onset of the monsoon once more.

1938 saw the last attempt on Everest from the north, made under the leadership of Tilman. This was a much smaller and less costly expedition than previous ones, but it also met the usual troubles of too much snow and a too early monsoon. It was forced to retreat without gaining the summit and no further attempts were made until after World War II.

The change in the political situation during 1959-60 resulted in Tibet becoming closed to westerners while Nepal was opened to them. Now that access to Everest had to be through Nepal, the only approach appeared to be through the Khumbu icefall and Western Cwm, which Mallory had seen during the 1921 Reconnaissance Expedition. Although it seemed doubtful that a route could be found, there was no other choice.

In 1951 a full scale British reconnaissance expedition was sent by the Joint Everest Committee to examine the south side. It was led by Eric Shipton, and included Edmund Hillary and a physicist Tom Bourdillon, who with his father produced the oxygen apparatus used during the successful attack in 1953. This expedition pioneered the route through the treacherous Khumbu Icefall to reach the Western Cwm, the upper basin of the glacier.

Led by Dr Wyss Dunant in 1952, the Swiss made the first attempt via the Western Cwm and the South Col, after successfully negotiating the

Khumbu Icefall. Raymond Lambert and Tenzing Norgay Sherpa reached 28,200 feet (8597 metres), before having to turn back. Tenzing has said *"We could have gone further. We could perhaps have gone to the top. But we would not have come down again"*.

Another Swiss attempt was made in November of the same year, with Dr Chevally as leader and Lambert and Tenzing again in the climbing team. In spite of the prohibitive cold and wind of the post-monsoon weather, a height of 26,575 feet (8102 metres) was reached before the attempt was abandoned. Although these two expeditions were unsuccessful they did provide invaluable knowledge for future attempts.

The next year, 1953, the British Expedition led by John Hunt was successful in putting two men on the coveted summit: Edmund Hillary and Tenzing Norgay Sherpa. It was a fine achievement with no serious accidents or lives lost. The equipment used was the finest procurable at the time and much of it was specially designed for the expedition. The most crucial part of the whole climb was the ascent of the Lhotse face to gain the windswept South Col, from where a summit bid could be made. The first attempt by Evans and Bourdillon was not successful, although they did reach the South Summit at 28,700 feet (8750 metres). It was too far from the South Col to reach the top and return safely so a further camp was established at 27,900 feet (8506 metres); and from it the successful ascent was made on May the 29th.

The second successful ascent was made in 1956 by a Swiss expedition, and in 1963 the Americans completed the first traverse. Willi Unsoeld and Tom Hornbein ascended part of the previously unclimbed West Ridge, which forms the border between Tibet and Nepal, to reach the summit. The descent became a nightmare when, caught out by darkness they were forced to bivouac at 28,000 feet (8536 metres) without tents, oxygen, sleeping bags or food. Although the temperature dropped to minus 18 degrees Fahrenheit there was no wind. The gods must surely have been smiling as they would have undoubtably perished if the usual Everest weather had prevailed. It was the highest night out ever spent on a mountain.

First Ascents of other major Khumbu Peaks

Lhotse 8501 metres. Swiss, 18th May 1956. Ernst Reiss and Fritz Luchsinger.
Lhotse Shar 8383 metres. 1970. Austrian. S. Mayerl and R. Walter.
Nuptse 7879 metres. British, 1961. D. Davis, Tashi
next day — C. Bonington, L. Brown J. Swallow, Ang Pemba
Ama Dablam 6856 metres. New Zealand, 13th March 1961. Mike Ward, Mike Gill, Wally Romanes, Barry Bishop
Tawoche 6367 metres. New Zealand, March 1963. Jim Wilson, Mike Gill, Dave Dornan, Ang Temba
Kangtaiga 6779 metres. New Zealand, 5th June 1963. Jim Wilson, Mike Gill, Dave Dornan.
Tamserku 6608 metres. New Zealand, 11th November 1964. Pete Farrell, R. Stewart, John McKinnon, Lyn Crawford.
Pumori 7145 metres. German 1962. G. Lenser, V. Huereemann, H. Ruetzel, E. Farrer.
Cho Oyo 8153 metres. Swiss 1954. S. Joechler, H. Tichy, Passang Dawa Lama.
Gyachung Kang 7922 metres. Japanese 1964. Y. Kato, K. Sakaizawa, Passang Phutar III.

With the route to the South Col now the standard one, and the West Ridge climbed as well, mountaineers turned their attention to the Southwest Face. The first attempt was made by the Japanese in the spring of 1970, after a reconnaissance the previous year. The expedition also made a successful simultaneous attempt by the usual route. Unfortunately, climbers on the Southwest Face were injured by rock fall and the attempt was abandoned.

The next attempt on the Southwest Face came the following spring by the 1971 International Expedition. Although large and with many famous climbers, the expedition failed to scale the face, mainly because of lack of co-operation between its members. 1972 saw another two attempts; the unsuccessful European Expedition in the spring, and one in the autumn led by Chris Bonington. This was also beaten back by a combination of high winds and the extreme cold of the post-monsoon period.

The Japanese tried unsuccessfully again in the autumn of 1973, and Bonington's next attempt came in 1975. This time he was successful and the Southwest Face was climbed.

With the summit traversed and the Southwest Face climbed, there still remained the challenge of climbing Everest without oxygen. Many people thought it would be impossible but they were proved wrong when two members of the spring 1978 Austrian Expedition, Rheinhold Messner and Peter Habeler, reached the summit without its aid. Messner's triumph was repeated in August 1980 when he ascended to the summit alone, again without oxygen but this time from the northern side.

Since the first attempts before World War II the original route from the north has been used again, by the Chinese who claimed a successful ascent on 25th May 1960. This success has never been proved and accounts of the ascent leave some doubts. In 1975 the Chinese claimed the second woman to have reached the top. The first, only a few days earlier, was Mrs Junko Tabei with Sherpa Ang Tsering, of the Japanese Women's Expedition. Since then three other women have reached the summit.

Although part of the West Ridge was climbed by the Americans in 1963, when they traversed the summit, the full length of this ridge was not attempted until the spring of 1979. A large Yugoslavian Expedition successfully climbed the entire West Ridge from the Lho La to the summit.

This was another major achievement. For Ang Phu Sherpa, sirdar for this expedition, it was his second ascent to the summit, by a different route each time, but unfortunately he was killed during the descent. Another Sherpa, Nawang Gombu, was the first person to reach the top twice with his second ascent in 1965, both times by the Southeast Ridge.

The first winter ascent was made in February 1980 by Lezek Cichy and Krystof Wielicki of Poland. The severe cold experienced by these men when ascending to over 8000 metres at that time of the year needs no imagination.

On 5 May 1988, world attention focused once more on Everest with the first live-telecast of a summit success, by members of the China-Japan-Nepal Friendship Expedition. A total of twelve climbers — three Nepalese, four Chinese and five Japanese — reached the summit, making the largest number of people to reach the top in a single day. Two teams, of three each, ascended from opposite sides, met at the top, then descended the other's paths, thus completing the first-ever North to South, South to North, and double traverses. Five days later, two more Nepalese from this expedition made another successful climb.

There are now over fifteen attempts each year to climb Everest, by different routes on both sides and during all seasons. Expeditions must apply for permits several years ahead.

Not only is Everest the highest mountain in the world, but it has also claimed more lives than any other peak in the Nepal Himalaya.

The rising number of deaths, resulting in many families being left without a wage-earner, has made many Sherpas reluctant to go on expeditions, so the trend now is towards smaller climbing parties using fewer porters and no Sherpas beyond the base camps. The rise in popularity of trekking, with its easier lifestyle, has attracted many Sherpas to engage in the tourist business where the financial gains are as good and the chances of survival better. Some Sherpas, though, have become climbers in their own right and find the challenges of mountaineering and the achievement of summits a goal in itself.

George Leigh Mallory, a member of the 1922 and 1924 British Everest Expeditions. He was probably the first European to view the Khumbu region when he reached the Lho La from the Tibetan side.

The first expeditions to attempt to climb Sagarmatha had this view of their goal, from 5500 metres on the Rongbuk Glacier, as they approached from the northern side.

A Journey of Discovery

Towards Sagarmatha

There are only two ways to reach Sagarmatha National Park — by walking, or by taking a forty minute flight from Kathmandu with the Royal Nepal Airlines Corporation into Lukla Airstrip, and then walking several kilometres up the Dudh Kosi Valley to the Park entrance. Detailed guides of walking routes can be found in a variety of trekking books available in Kathmandu and around the world. Most walking routes to the Park take between ten and fourteen days. Bookings for the flight into Lukla can be made through trekking agencies or at the Royal Nepal Airline Corporation Offices on the corner of New Road in Kathmandu.

Lukla at 2850 metres is south of Khumbu in the area known as Pharak and is perched above the Dudh Kosi River on a broad terrace.

Leaving Lukla the trail descends gradually, passing above the large village of Chaunrikaka and on through small villages, fields and forests, following a wide well constructed path. After Kusum Drangka, a large side stream, the trail crosses the Dudh Kosi at Phakding then follows the western bank, passing through forests of blue pine until it reaches the small village of Benkar. Beyond this village the trail crosses to the eastern bank of the Dudh Kosi beside a large rock with excellent examples of mani carving on it, and climbs gently to the village of Chumoa. Between here and the the next village of Monjo the trail drops steeply to cross the Kyashar, or Monjo Khola, which is fed by the mountains of Tamserku, Kangtaiga and Kusum Kangurru.

It is here at Monjo that most visitors enter Sagarmatha National Park, and at 2800 metres this is about the Park's lowest point. Park entrance fees are paid here. From Monjo the trail crosses a small saddle behind a rock buttress, then descends to Jorsalle, the last village before Namche Bazar.

Beyond Jorsalle the trail climbs high above bluffs on the eastern side of the valley, eventually dropping steeply into the Dudh Kosi gorge, just above the confluence of the Bhote Kosi. From the bridge there are good views of Mt Tawoche, framed between the steep rock walls of the gorge. Because of their steepness and inaccessibility, the cold shaded, eastern slopes of the valley are densely vegetated with firs and bamboo, the habitat of Red Pandas. Anyone passing through here very early in the morning or at dusk may be fortunate enough to see one of these handsome animals.

From Monjo, set in pine forest at the lowest point and entrance to the Park, Khumbi-yul-lha mountain appears ahead like the watchful guardian local people believe it to be.

Starting point of many journeys, Lukla airstrip is about a day's walk from the Park entrance.

In contrast, the dry, sunny western slopes of the Dudh Kosi are clothed sparsely with Blue Pines. From the bridge the trail climbs steeply, following ledges between bluffs until the crest of the ridge separating the Bhote Kosi and Dudh Kosi valleys is reached. Vistas up the Dudh Kosi valley give the first views of Sagarmatha, rising above the wall of Nuptse and Lhotse. The trail now crosses to the other side of the ridge and climbs more gently, traversing above the Bhote Kosi until Namche Bazar is reached. Namche is a thriving village with many Sherpa hotels offering a variety of accommodation, and shops which stock an interesting assortment of foodstuffs, trekking and mountaineering equipment, clothing, souvenirs and fabrics.

As the name suggests, Namche Bazar is a market town, and every Saturday morning the traders, mostly Rai or Tamang people from the south and east, arrive from lower altitudes. Some have carried their loads of rice, wheat, or millet for up to seven days to reach Namche. They find it cold in the early morning while waiting for trading to begin, and sit huddled in groups for warmth, often around tiny fires. Eggs, meat, fruit and vegetables can also be purchased at times.

Once trading begins, it is usually brisk, and the market place becomes crowded with jostling Sherpas who have come from all the villages in the Park to get their supplies. Some of them have had to walk for one or two days to get to the market and must later return to their homes with their heavy purchases. By midday most of the trading is over, and the traders stride off downhill with their empty baskets bouncing freely. Meanwhile the Sherpas make the most of their visit to Namche and Saturday becomes the social day of the week, with the chang and teashops well patronised.

The market place is a terraced area beside a large rock, where the trail from Jorsalle enters the outskirts of the village. One hundred metres above is the Police Station, where trekkers must have their trekking permits checked. Higher above that is the small village school, then the Park Headquarters and Visitor Centre. On the opposite side of the village is the local *gompa* with its ochre-red walls.

Set in the sheltered, horseshoe-shaped basin high above the Bhote Kosi gorge, terraced houses of Namche shrug off a spring snowfall as warmth from the morning sun reaches them.

The end of a four day journey for many. Bowed under his heavy load this porter climbs the 600 metre hill to Namche, in time for the Saturday market.

Once there some bargain, while others sun themselves on a rock beside the market place.

Namche Bazar.

151

Having reached Namche, visitors now have a choice of places to visit. There are four major valleys in the Park: the Bhote Kosi, the traditional trading route to Tibet; the Dudh Kosi leading to the Ngozumpa Glacier, Gokyo Lake and Mt Cho Oyo; the main Khumbu Valley leading to the Everest Base Camp; and the Imja Valley running up under Nuptse and Lhotse, Baruntse and the rear of Ama Dablam. (These alternative routes are detailed in a further section).

From Namche, the main Everest trail at first ascends the hill past the Police Station to a cluster of houses in the saddle above, then traverses the steep slopes of the Dudh Kosi gorge. Along this comparatively barren stretch of trail, Himalayan Tahr, Impeyan Pheasants, soaring Griffons and Lammergeirs are often seen. The scene changes with every corner. From one prominent bend a spectacular view is gained of Mt Tawoche with remote Phortse Village perched on its flanks above the junction of the Dudh Kosi and Imja Khola. The Tengboche Monastery trail can be seen traversing the forested ridge which sweeps down from Mt Kangtaiga. Nearer is Teshinga, a large village with fields used mainly in the summer for growing potatoes. Below is the river, more easily seen from here where the gorge opens out a little.

Ahead is a small side valley, where the trail leading down from Khunde and Khumbjung villages joins the main trekking route in the streambed.

This area of mixed rhododendron, birch and silver fir forest brings relief from the bare hillsides of the gorge, and a cautious, quiet approach to it may reward you. Musk deer and Impeyan Pheasants are often seen around here. Just after the Khunde/Khumbjung trail junction are the teashops of Sarnasa, a customary place for Tibetan traders to sit with their ornaments and souvenirs displayed on cloths spread beside the trail. They will encourage you to buy as many of their wares as possible, but remember — bargaining is traditional and expected.

Beyond Sarnasa on a prominent, stepped corner, it is possible to look back down into a very narrow section of the gorge to where a huge boulder is wedged between the rock walls. The vegetation growing on top of this boulder prior to the 1977 flood, was swept away by the water but the boulder remained unmoved. From here the trail descends to the river, passing below Teshinga through a pleasant pine forest. One of the tree nurseries established by the New Zealand Nepal bi-lateral aid project to assist the Sherpa people with reafforestation can be seen here. Owing to modifications by the 1977 flood, the river banks here are in an unstable condition, but an excellent bridge now spans the torrent. Immediately upstream from the bridge is the confluence of the Dudh Kosi and the Imja Khola, both rivers emerging from narrow gorges.

On the terrace above the eastern bank are the teashops, hotels and National Park Guard Post of Phunki Tenga. As this settlement is at 3250 metres which is quite low in the Park, it is a good place to retreat to if affected by altitude sickness. A row of prayer wheels lines the stream outside the hotels.

Dominating the scenery, spectacular and beautiful Ama Dablam, meaning "Mother's Charmbox", takes its name from the bulge of ice which hangs from the upper mountain face, between the two flanks or shoulders.

The surrounding forest is in reasonable condition and not as heavily modified as in other places by the gathering of firewood and grazing of animals, but even so is beginning to show signs of overuse. Tengboche Monastery is about 600 metres above Phunki Tenga on the long spur reaching down from Kangtaiga.

From Phunki Tenga the trail at first zig-zags up through thick forest, then sidles out into more open country, climbing gradually towards the top of the ridge. Adjacent to the monastery is a large hotel run by the monks, while along the ridge to the left and rear is the trekker's lodge built as part of the New Zealand Project contribution. The view from the ridge above the monastery is superb, with a panorama of the surrounding mountains, both up and down the valley. Sagarmatha towers above the imposing wall of Nuptse and Lhotse, and Ama Dablam thrusts upwards, dominating all. The trail to Phortse and Gokyo can be seen threading across the slopes of Khumbi-yul-lha and up the high slopes of the Dudh Kosi Valley.

Crossing the grassed area in front of the monastery, the trail descends through forest to a long terrace. Tame blood pheasants are frequently seen in large flocks along this section of trail. The nun's settlement of Devoche is tucked among the juniper trees and at the far end of the terrace is Milingo, another small religious settlement.

After passing Milingo, the river is recrossed on a suspension bridge over a spectacular narrow gorge, and the trail then climbs upwards around ledges and bluffs to a chorten and entranceway at a small saddle beside a rocky outcrop. Immediately after this saddle the trail branches: the left one leading uphill to Upper Pangboche village and the right one to Lower Pangboche. Both Upper and Lower Pangboche are fair-sized villages. Upper Pangboche has a *gompa* which is thought to be the oldest in the region, and it is here that one of the yeti relics is housed. A grove of very tall juniper trees surrounding this *gompa* is probably the best stand of this tree left in the Park. A remnant of the forest which once covered much of the hillsides, they are protected by their proximity to the *gompa*.

Bathed in early morning sunlight, the golden finial atop the chorten at Tengboche reflects the glory of its surroundings.

Shelter and safe habitat for many birds and animals, birch forest clothes the hillside between Tengboche, Devoche and Milingo Villages.

In the main valley just above Pangboche, is a small lake which was formed in 1977 when flood waters rushed down the Nare Drangka opposite and temporarily blocked the Imja Khola. It is slowly being silted up with material brought down by the river and will no doubt disappear in time. From Pangboche the trail maintains height for a while, not far above the Imja Khola, then climbs again through the small group of houses of Shomare. The height gained to Shomare is maintained and travel continues along a broad terrace. As the confluence of the Imja and Lobuche Khola is neared there is another junction in the trail. The one to the right continues down to the confluence and then up to Dingboche in the Imja Valley. Dingboche is the highest permanently settled area and is noted for producing the best quality barley for tsampa.

To reach Pheriche the left trail up the hillside is taken, passing above some houses and over a shoulder before descending and crossing the Khumbu Khola. This valley is wide and flat until it curves to the right and rises up onto the terminal moraine of the Khumbu Glacier. Pheriche is at the lower end of this flat and is comprised mainly of Sherpa hotels and teashops. The distinctive feature of the village is the use of rocks and turf for the construction of walls, giving them a brown and white striped appearance. Utilisation of the turf has resulted in the absence of topsoil around the village, where timber and firewood are used sparingly. Pheriche was once only a summer settlement (*yersa*) but with the influx of trekkers it is now a permanent village providing very basic accommodation. A surprising amount and variety of imported foodstuffs can be purchased here, all of it left by mountaineering expeditions. There is also the Himalayan Rescue Association first-aid post which usually functions during the trekking season, from October until April. As an alternative to the Sherpa Hotels there is a trekkers lodge similar to that at Tengboche. Tracks leading to Dingboche climb the hillside above Pheriche and cross the low moraine ridges which separate the Khumbu and Imja Valleys.

From Pheriche the first part of the route to Lobuche passes up the long scrubby river flats to the walled fields of Phulong Karpo. After this settlement the terrain rises gradually and the trail climbs to a gentle trough above the river. It follows this for a short distance, then drops down and crosses to the western bank and the teashops of Duglha. The increase in altitude is obvious here. It is in this region and beyond that the effects of altitude sickness may become apparent. They should not be taken lightly and any symptoms such as headaches should be heeded.

The terminal moraine of the Khumbu Glacier is just above, and a long steady climb to the top brings panoramic views of the route already travelled and that to come. A row of *chortens* in memory of Sherpas and climbers killed during attempts on Sagarmatha marks the top of the climb, the nearby stone walls making a good resting place before continuing. From here the trail follows the small valley and stream bed on the left side of the moraine wall. Lobuche is found tucked in a sheltered corner at the base of the Lobuche Glacier which descends from Mt Lobuche directly above. There are a few Sherpa hotels here providing basic accommodation and a variety of foodstuffs. The highest of the N.Z. Project trekkers' lodges, constructed to help ease the shortage of accommodation during peak trekking times, is in this settlement.

In silent remembrance a row of chortens, near the top of the Khumbu moraine, commemorates the deaths of those killed while attempting to climb Sagarmatha. They are as peaceful as Ama Dablam appears, gleaming in the late sunlight across the valley, but a subtle reminder to all who pass of the vulnerability of man.

Walled fields at Pheriche pattern river flats of the Khumbu valley before it curves right toward the terminal moraine of its glacier. The moraine entering to the left is from the Tshola Glacier beneath Tawoche and Cholatse.

The illusionary warmth of first sunlight breaks the cold grip of night as it creeps down the mountainside to trekkers' tents and Sherpa huts at Lobuche. Once just a grazing area used only in summer by yak herders, Lobuche is now occupied for most of the year by trekkers, and Sherpa hosts who have turned their small dwellings into accommodation.

From Lobuche the route continues up the grassy valley beside the Khumbu Glacier moraine, climbing gradually until the terminal moraine of the Changri Nup and Changri Shar Glaciers is reached.. A steep climb is made to the top of this moraine, and then the trail undulates across moraine rubble until a final short descent is made to the dry, sandy area of Gorak Shep with its shallow lake beyond. Rising above Gorak Shep is a grassy hill, Kala Pattar, and from here the view of Sagarmatha, the Khumbu Icefall and Glacier, Nuptse and other peaks makes the effort of the climb worthwhile. Symmetrical Mt Pumori rises above, seeming no more than a stone's throw away.

After leaving the head of the lake at Gorak Shep the trail climbs through an area of large boulders on which are plaques and engravings in memory of some of the many climbers and Sherpas who have died while climbing in this area. The trail then crosses the moraine wall and descends to the Khumbu Glacier. Snowfalls, exposure and avalanche winds can prove hazardous, the glacier and Base Camp not being regarded as a general trekking area. Cairns mark the route across the rubble but these shift with the movement of the ice so it is constantly changing. It is not difficult to lose the semblance of a trail and care is needed. In the centre of the glacier is a broad, rubble-covered ridge which the general route follows towards the Lho La, the obvious pass ahead. The Base Camp is situated on the ice near the foot of the Khumbu Icefall at an altitude of 5400 metres.

Expeditions are usually in residence from August to late October for post-monsoon climbs, and February to May for pre-monsoon attempts. As the expeditions have limited resources and are under some strain, visitors are not always welcome. It is advisable to be fully self-sufficient for a night on, and in icy conditions. Although expeditions can not stop people from visiting the Base Camp area, some erect signs warning that visitors are not welcome.

From the Base Camp the summits of Nuptse, Lhotse and Sagarmatha are lost from sight. The dominant feature of the landscape is the Khumbu Icefall. Like the ruins of a gigantic city it cascades between the ramparts of Sagarmatha and Nuptse in a chaos of ice masonary. Huge towers and blocks jumbled, slowly toppling, cracking and groaning as they move relentlessly downwards. It is the ladder up which most expeditions choose to climb to reach the coveted summit of Sagarmatha, separating the mountaineer from the trekker.

Not everyone is welcome at the Base Camp site as this sign clearly warns. Often under stress themselves, some expeditions have found the pressure from visiting trekkers, who expect food and accommodation, has become intolerable.

...metrical and serene, Pumori, the "Daughter [Mo]untain" captures late sunlight while evening [sha]dows deepen below. Insignificant at the [ba]se of her central ridge is the rock capped hill [kn]own as Kala Pattar, the goal of most visitors [see]king a view of Sagarmartha.

The Park Headquarters and Visitor Centre on the hill above Namche Bazar provides a central focus for the Park, and opportunities for visitors to seek advice from park staff and learn about the natural and human history of the area.

Other Places to Visit

Mendelphu Hill and Park Visitor Centre

From Namche village the summit of Sagarmatha is not visible. A superb view can be had, however, from the rounded hill called Mendelphu, above the village. A walk to the Park Headquarters and Visitor Centre on the top of this hill is an excellent way to learn more about the Park while spending a day in Namche for acclimatisation. Paths to the Visitor Centre leave the main trails out of the village above the Police Checkpost and school, near a cluster of houses in the saddle. One path leads directly to the top of Mendelphu; the other traverses the hillside first, with good views down the Dudh Kosi Valley.

From the Visitor Centre there is a 360° view of the mountains of Khumbu, and the sun can be seen rising or setting on the highest point on earth. The Visitor Centre, built in 1978 by the New Zealand Government as part of the bi-lateral Aid Agreement to establish the Park, contains many interesting displays on the natural and human history of the Khumbu area. Adjacent buildings include offices and accommodation for Park staff and military personnel, a library and facilities for research. Allow one or two hours for the return trip from Namche.

Khunde and Khumbjung Villages

The twin villages of Khunde and Khumbjung nestle in a broad shallow trough beneath the southern slopes of Mt Khumbi-yul-lha, about 350 metres higher than Namche. Although they lack the tourist facilities available in Namche, these villages have a quiet charm. A night spent in either is worthwhile and can help in becoming acclimatised to the altitude. The adjacent forested areas are very beautiful with a network of paths within and around them. Bird life is rich and there is the possibility of seeing wild animals as well.

From Namche the Khunde/Khumbjung trail climbs out of the village to the *Gompa*, then takes a right-hand turn and climbs steeply up the hillside until it reaches the edge of Syangboche Airstrip. The airstrip was constructed to service the Hotel Everest View, built in 1971. From the time it was opened until about mid 1981 there were regular flights into Syangboche, bringing guests and supplies to the hotel, but now its future is unknown.

The trail crosses the top of the airstrip and climbs the hillside for a short distance to a stone *mani* wall and resting place. Here it divides, the left trail going to Khunde and the right one to Khumbjung and the Hotel Everest View, as follows.

To Khunde: The left trail sidles around the western side of the Government Yak Farm and climbs over a low saddle before descending to Khunde Village. There is a small hospital here, built by Sir Edmund Hillary and the Himalayan Trust. It was built primarily to help the Sherpa people, but it does extend help to trekkers with serious medical problems.

To Hotel Everest View: Above the *mani* wall, the right-hand trail divides again just before reaching a large *chorten* a little further up the hill. The trail to the hotel leads off to the right again (with the Khumbjung trail ahead) and sidles up across the hillside above the airstrip, crosses the ridge and

160

then turns left, traversing high above the Dudh Kosi Gorge until the hotel is reached. The grassy hilltops and mixed rhododendron and fir forest around the Hotel are magnificent. The view from here can only be described as superb.

Servicing a hotel of this size, at this altitude, was always a major problem for its owners and managers. As an example of excellent stonework, the exterior of this building is possibly the best in Khumbu, the other feature being its architecture which allows it to blend in with its surroundings. The lower end of Khumbjung village can be reached from the hotel by a trail which leads down from its western end, through the forest.

To Khumbjung: At the junction just before the *chorten*, the trail leads straight up the hillside and around the south-eastern side of the Yak Farm. It then crosses the low ridge and descends between boulders and forest to Khumbjung School on the outskirts of the village.

Rising directly behind Khunde and Khumbjung is Khumbi-yul-lha, the mountain which is most sacred to the Sherpas. On no account should visitors attempt to climb it. To the west of Khunde, descending from Khumbi-yul-lha is a long grassy ridge. The lower end can be gained by climbing left above the top of Syangboche airstrip. Alternatively, the upper end where it runs up to Khumbi-yul-lha mountain can be reached by taking the path immediately behind Khunde Hospital. The scenery from this ridge compensates for the effort of the climb up to it. On the western side is a steep drop down to the Bhote Kosi Valley with a view to Thami village perched above the junction of the Thengpo, while on the eastern side the Dudh Kosi is dominated by the peaks of Kangtaiga, Tamserku and Kusum Kangguru.

Another round trip can be made by travelling from Namche to the Hotel Everest View or the lower end of Khunde/Khumbjung villages and descending to the tea houses of Sarnasa, above the Dudh Kosi on the main Everest trail. The return trip is made via the main trail.

It is thought that a gigantic rockslide falling from Khumbi-yul-lha mountain thousands of years ago formed the low bouldery ridge which borders the shallow valley where Khunde and Khumbjung villages lie. Continued erosion of the mountain has slowly filled the valley with silt, creating the flat arable land now used by the Sherpas. These are clearly seen from the long ridge which decends from Khumbi-yul-lha.

Namche Bazar to Khumbjung, Khunde or the Hotel Everest View and return takes about four hours, while the trip via Sarnasa takes about five hours. All the day trips mentioned here are good for acclimatisation.

Bhote Kosi Valley and Thami Village

The walk to Thami Gompa takes about four hours, and the return journey can be made in one day but it is probably better to spend a night in Thami if time allows. This allows time for a short walk up towards Thengpo village, and to view the spectacular peaks of this area. Thami has not been exposed to trekkers and western culture to the same extent as villages on the Everest Base Camp trail, but food and accommodation are available.

From Namche the trail climbs above the village *gompa* and continues left to the eastern side of the Bhote Kosi Valley, staying high above the river. The steep sides of the gorge are forested with mixed fir, pines and rhododendrons until the valley opens out slightly. Along this section of trail the brilliant danphe pheasant is often seen and heard while the musk deer may also be glimpsed as it seeks cover amongst the trees. Just before the Kyajo Drangka, a hanging valley which drains the western flank of Mt Khumbi-yul-lha, is a small forest of rhododendrons and birch trees, a particularly beautiful area from late April onwards when the spring flowers of rhododendrons, primulas and iris are prolific. After crossing the Kyajo the trail sidles around a spur, and the village of Thamo, with its grove of large rhododendron trees, can be seen ahead. Trails up this spur lead to Louda *gompa* perched high on the hillside overlooking Thamo and the Bhote Kosi.

Thamo was the site for a small hydro-electric scheme, partially financed by the Austrian Government, to provide electricity for Namche Bazar. Work started on this project in 1979 but in 1986 a devastating flood, caused when a glacial lake drained suddenly, destroyed most of the construction and altered the site. A new site further up the valley will now be used.

Leaving Thamo, the trail passes through open country, often diverting to pass fine examples of mani stones, until it descends and crosses the Bhote Kosi. It then climbs steadily on the western bank, sidling into the Thengpo Khola through a mixed rhododendron and juniper forest to come out by the potato fields of Lower Thami. Just below the fields the trail divides, the left branch leading into the village and fields, and the right one continuing up onto a low ridge dividing the Thengpo from the Bhote Kosi. The view up both valleys is good from this ridge which is an old moraine wall. Upper Thami, where there is a National Park Guard Post, is a little further up the Bhote Kosi on its western side, just beyond the Police Checkpost. Visitors are restricted from travelling beyond Upper Thami towards the Nangpa La without special permits, because this is a sensitive border area with Chinese Tibet.

The trail continues up the ridge, where it is joined by other trails from the fields of Lower Thami on the left, and Upper Thami on the right, then it climbs to Thami Monastery which is built into the steep, bluffed hillside high above the Thengpo Khola. Thami Monastery is one of the main centres of Buddhism in the Park and is still relatively unaffected by tourism. Across the Thengpo the sheer walls rise to Mt Kongde and Teng Kangpoche, as the valley curves around and up towards the Tashi Lhabtsa Pass. From the monastery the trail traverses around the hillside, fairly high above the river, passing through shrubby junipers and rhododendrons until it comes out on the grassy river flats below the summer village of Thengpo. It then continues up the northern side of the valley, along terraces, until the first rubble of the moraine is reached. From here the trail becomes indistinct, marked only by infrequent cairns as it climbs up through the moraine to the ice. Tashi Lhabtsa at its head is a high pass, and anyone attempting to cross it must be well acclimatised to the altitude, experienced in mountaineering and accompanied by an experienced Sherpa guide.

Massive ramparts and walls support the Thami Gompa and the monastery houses which merge with the steep bluffs they shelter beneath, high above the Thengpo river. These buildings provide a blending between the natural environment and man's need for shelter — an element that is often overlooked in the western world.

The fields of Lower Thami lie near the end of the Thengpo Valley, below an ancient, curving moraine wall where trails lead up to the monastery. As the valley narrows, its sheer walls curve around to Tashi Lhabtsa, a high pass at the head which provides experienced climbers with access to the Rolwaling Valley.

Dudh Kosi Valley and Gokyo Lake

This valley does not receive the attention of visitors as much as it deserves for it is an excellent alternative to the Everest Base Camp area.

There are several small settlements on both sides of the valley but they are only used in summer, when cattle are taken up for grazing on the high pastures.

At the foot of the ridge on which Tengboche Monastery is located is the confluence of the Dudh Kosi River, which drains the great glaciers below Mt's Cho Oyo and Gyachung Kang in the north, and the equally big Imja Khola descending from the Sagarmatha and Lhotse-Nuptse massif to the north-east. Above this confluence the Dudh Kosi has cut a spectacular gorge between the mountains of Tawoche and Khumbi-yul-lha. Isolated by this gorge, remote Phortse village is perched on a sunny terrace on the lower slopes of Mt Tawoche. As the slopes immediately above the gorge are too steep for a trail, the route to Phortse first climbs high under Khumbi-yul-lha mountain before descending to cross the Dudh Kosi above the gorge entrance. The final climb from the river to the village is through a magnificent birch forest.

The main route from Namche, up the Dudh Kosi, is followed until the teashops at Sarnasa. At this point the trail to Phortse, coming from Khumbjung, traverses the hillside high above the teashops.

It can be gained by taking a small path leading straight uphill from behind the teashops. There is a junction in the Phortse trail above the teashops but

Contrasting day and night temperatures during winter cause streams to flow briefly during the day and freeze at night, creating frozen cascades like this beside the trail to Gokyo.

164

either route can be taken. The lower route to the right is wider and less steep, and is suitable for cattle, while the left one climbs steeply up to bluffs above, then ascends rock steps through a narrow chimney to emerge onto the grassy slopes above. This route is for people only and is slightly quicker.

The paths rejoin further on before reaching a large *chorten* at a high point of 3973 metres. From the *chorten* the trail descends in switch-backs through mixed scrub and forest towards the river, with spectacular views down into the gorge. From the river, at about 3500 metres, there is a choice of routes up the valley. By crossing the river and climbing up through Phortse Village the trail up the eastern side can be taken. These slopes are generally steep, and apart from fields around the summer village of Konar (one hour's walk above Phortse) there are very few camping sites. The western side of the valley offers easier travelling and numerous campsites.

From the river the trail up the western side climbs through mixed fir and birch forest, rising steeply in places around bluffs, with many waterfalls which will be frozen during the winter and spring months. The first summer village reached is Dole, in a small side valley. From here the trail continues up a grass and scrub-covered hillside, past the few houses of Gyele, to Lhabharma. Water is only available at Lhabharma during the wet summer months.

Most of the climbing is over for a while, and from Lhabharma the trail continues at much the same level to Luza, situated in another small side valley. From Luza a further gentle climb over undulating country brings a view up into the wide Machhermo Valley with its glaciated head and surrounding peaks. At Machhermo the stream is crossed, and the trail veers back towards the main Dudh Kosi Valley, crossing a low ridge to a flat terrace holding the scattered houses of Pangka. Opposite this settlement is the terminal moraine of the Ngozumpa Glacier. Several small yersa can be seen across the valley.

From Pangka the trail drops to river level then runs alongside it, around bluffs, and up on to the terminal moraine. Near the top of the moraine the stream is crossed on rough stone blocks, and the trail climbs into the valley to the left. The first small lake is soon passed and then a second, larger lake is reached. At its top end, a few rough stone walls and the remains of some houses are all there is to Longponga. The trail continues up the stream until the third lake and Gokyo village with its collection of low-roofed houses and walled fields is reached.

Gokyo village is beside the third of five lakes tucked in against the lateral moraine of the Ngozumpa Glacier, with the fourth and largest lake about another hour's walk further up the valley. The steep hill rising directly above the northern end of Gokyo is known as Gokyo Ri, and from its top there are impressive views of Sagarmatha, Makalu, Gyachung Kang and numerous other peaks. Narrow paths also lead around the northern end of the lake to large grassy basins at its head. For the less energetic a short climb to the top of the moraine wall behind the houses gives a different but almost as rewarding view of Cho Oyo, the world's seventh highest mountain, its great snow-covered bulk giving rise to the massive Ngozumpa Glacier. Across to the southeast are the impressively steep summits of Cholatse and Tawoche. Gokyo is at an altitude of 4750 metres. At least two days are needed to travel there from Namche or Khumbjung, but to allow for better acclimatisation, three days are recommended.

For the return trip to Phortse via the eastern side of the Dudh Kosi, it is best to cross the moraine of the Ngozumpa Glacier to Tarnak (Dragnag on some maps) which lies at the southern end of some dark bluffs. There is a cairned route across the moraine, leading from the lower end of the second lake which was passed on the way up to Gokyo. Although the grass area from the lake is not well marked there is a marker cairn on top of a low section of the moraine wall. From this cairn the trail across the rubble of the moraine is reasonably clear.

From Tarnak the route down the eastern side travels across pleasant open country, passing small *yersa,* then descends near to the river when opposite the Machermo Valley. The river is then left behind as the trail climbs steadily, sidling around steep hillsides and passing occasional houses perched above the river, until a high point marked by a *chorten* is reached. From the *chorten* there is a descent to the village of Konar in a side valley, and a further traverse around the steep slopes of the Dudh Kosi to reach the upper limits of Phortse.

There is a choice of routes out of Phortse, other than the one from Khumbjung or Namche, and both are interesting alternatives. One leads from the upper, northern edge of the village and traverses steep slopes high above the Imja Khola, opposite Tengboche Monastery, to Upper Pangboche village. This trail is a marvellous work of engineering, crossing very steep rock bluffs in places. The other trail, leading from the upper, southern corner of Phortse, nearest the Imja Khola, descends into its gorge. The Imja is crossed by a good wooden bridge, then the trail climbs directly up through forest to emerge by Tengboche Monastery.

Morning mists and shadows lie over the moraine of the Ngozumpa Glacier, which descends from Cho Oyo, the world's seventh highest mountain.

Suspended high above the junction of the Dudh Kosi and Imja Khola, chortens mark where the terraced fields of Phortse end. Below the fields slopes fall abruptly to cold waters tumbling through the gorges, and the valley opens away to the distance beyond.

Imja Valley

Dingboche Village, at the lower end of the Imja Valley, is reached either from Pheriche or the trail at the confluence of the Khumbu and Imja Khola. From this confluence the trail climbs steadily above the Imja Khola to some terraces, then crosses a low ridge. The houses and fields of this high village are spread out over a wide alluvial terrace, and the trail threads its way between stone walls to the hillside at the northern edge. A spring-fed stream flows down or alongside the trail through the village making it muddy in places. Near a small *chorten* marking where the stream descends from the hillside are some hotel/teashops.

To reach Chukong, the summer village and grazing area further up the valley, the trail around the northern edge of the village is followed until the walled fields end. It continues on this side of the valley to the houses of Bibre, which are just past a large sidestream descending from the north. Terraces after Bibre are followed, then the trail crosses bouldery undulating ground, climbing gradually all the time. Chukong is a pleasant open area at the base of three major glaciers flowing down from Nuptse and Lhotse. Principally a summer grazing village, there are a few dwellings, and food and accommodation are available. The return trip to Chukong, from Pheriche or Dingboche, can easily be done in a day. The walk is a good way to acclimatise.

The route from Chukong to the Island Peak Base Camp veers first south, then up onto the top of a moraine ridge which it follows eastward for a short while before descending to a wide, open area between the moraines of the Imja and Lhotse Glaciers. At the top of this open area is the terminal moraine of the Imja Glacier, and by turning north and following a short small gully at its base, a wide, open, silted lake bed is reached. This is crossed, or skirted around, and the valley leading east at the left side of the Imja Glacier is followed up to Island Peak.

An alternative to the Island Peak Base Camp is the area under Amphu Lhabtsa, a high pass leading into the Hunku Valley. The Imja Glacier can be crossed below Island Peak, or an easier route is to travel up the moraine ridge on the southern edge. A deep circular lake is passed, and then grassy slopes and a small valley are reached. By climbing the slopes above this small valley and heading south, a terrace leading further up into the Amphu basin is reached. On an even higher terrace is a series of beautiful small lakes. The views across the valley to Island Peak, Nuptse, Lhotse and the head of the Imja are magnificent.

Green summer crops contrast with snowy peaks and glaciers of the Imja Valley. At 4400 metres Dingboche is the highest permanent village in the Park, and barley grown in its irrigated fields is judged to be the best in Khumbu.

Reflecting vivid colour from a clear blue sky the azure water of a moraine lake in the upper Imja Valley contrasts dramatically with surrounding rock and snow.

Returning Down-Valley

An alternative, longer route back to Pangboche from Dingboche or Pheriche can be taken down the south-eastern side of the Imja Khola. There is a bridge across the Imja near the upper end of Dingboche village, but trails from it down the south-eastern side to its confluence with the Lobuche Khola are vague, and travel is rough. But there is another bridge, a single plank only, across the Imja immediately above the confluence. Good trails from here can be followed down this side of the valley. There is a short climb to the village of Ralha, then the trail skirts the upper edge of the birch forest, eventually descending back to river level. The Imja can be recrossed here and the main trail to Pangboche is regained by a short climb. From this route the views gained give a different perspective of the peaks and the valley systems.

If the up-valley route has been via Tengboche, then the return to Namche from Pangboche can be made via Phortse village. This again takes longer than the standard route but is worth doing. Trails to and from Phortse are described under the section on the Dudh Kosi Valley and Gokyo Lake.

As well as the main valleys and routes described here there are innumerable trails to summer villages and grazing areas. These can all be explored, and new vistas revealed.

169

Preparations
Clothing
Any comprehensive trekking guide will give a complete list of clothes to bring, but the following will give a general idea.

The climate of the Park is mainly sunny and dry but cold, particularly at night, so warm down-filled or padded dacron jackets are almost essential if you are planning to be there between November and March. There are numerous places in Kathmandu which sell and hire suitable clothing and other trekking equipment.

Winds can be unpleasantly strong and cold at times above Tengboche, so a light-weight, windproof, outer jacket is useful. A jacket that is rainproof as well as windproof will be ideal.

Comfortable trousers, or a skirt for women, are generally adequate during the day, but woollen or thermal underwear, or padded overpants will probably be needed at night. A woollen hat and mittens or gloves are necessary.

Most trekkers find a combination of lightweight boots and a pair of running or tennis shoes are all that is necessary for walking and wearing around camp. Heavy boots are only needed if you are planning to go off the main trails and onto the glaciers or snow. Warm woollen socks are better than nylon or cotton ones.

Other Comforts
Suncreams and sunglasses are essential. The sunlight is very intense at high altitudes and can burn quickly. A fresh fall of snow intensifies the light making sunglasses necessary to avoid snowblindness.

If you are susceptible to fleas then flea powder should be included in your kit. There is nothing more irritating than an elusive flea, with only its bites to prove its existence.

Another essential item is a good supply of effective, strong, throat and cough lozenges. Even the mildest cough or cold will become more severe because of the dry air and altitude.

Before you leave Home
Try to become as fit as possible before leaving home. You will enjoy your stay much more. A thorough medical check-up is essential, and anyone with a heart defect or pulmonary complaint should not contemplate visiting the area. The effects of high altitude can be severe; a person who is not well to start with risks ruining not only his own health and holiday but also the enjoyment of others he may be with.

Innoculations against cholera, typhoid, tetanus and poliomyelitis are recommended, and just before departure an injection of gamma globulin will help minimise the effects of hepatitis, if you are unfortunate enough to become ill with it. Hepatitis is a common complaint in Nepal.

Cultural Tips
Above all, respect the customs, traditions and rituals of the Sherpa people, no matter how obscure the reasons for them may appear to you. Their values will be different from yours and perhaps difficult for you to understand. The Sherpas certainly understand that western values differ from theirs and will try to overlook a trekker's acts of disrespect, unless

they feel that their gods have been offended. The following is a list of ethics that will help you to enjoy your stay, and make you more acceptable to a people whose homeland and hospitality you are enjoying.

Always walk on the left sides of *Mani* walls and stones as you pass them (your right arm next to the *mani*). This shows respect for an age-old tradition.

Do not climb *mani* rocks, sit on *mani* walls, or hang items of washing or clothing on them.

Do not take *mani* stones as souvenirs; removal from their place of offering is sacrilege.

Do not put items such as used tissues or food scraps in the fires of Sherpa hearths, because it is believed that offensive odours from such pollution anger the local mountain gods.

Try not to put dirty substances, including soap, into the local rivers and springs, because it is believed that this will anger the water spirit.

Do not attempt to climb Khumbi-yul-lha, the mountain directly behind Khunde and Khumbjung villages; this is the sacred abode of the protective deity of all Khumbu.

The name of a dead person should not be mentioned to his close relatives, or in his old house, as this may attract his reincarnated spirit. Many Sherpas do not allow whistling in their houses for the same reason. Do not write a Sherpa's name in red ink as this colour symbolises death and is used for inscriptions at funeral services.

Do not give to begging children, but do donate if approached by a begging monk or nun, as this is a time-honoured religious tradition. Children should not be given sweets as there has been a marked decline in the quality of Sherpas' teeth since tourism became established. If you wish to give small gifts, useful items such as pens, pencils, writing pads, sewing needles and towels are more appropriate.

Always make a small contribution of a few rupees to any temples or monasteries that you visit. This is a time-honoured local tradition. Ask permission to take photographs of people. If you are photographing extensively, it is polite to give the subjects a small gift such as the traditional bottle of chang.

If you offer food or drink to a Sherpa and he politely refuses, you should offer again, and yet again, as Sherpa hospitality rules require three offerings of *she, she, she* (pronounced Shay), and three ritual refusals of *me, me, me*. A traditional Sherpa will be very reluctant to accept something on the first offer.

Do not ask a Sherpa to kill an animal for you. This is forbidden in Khumbu, both by village social rules and also by the Buddhist religion.

Women should not expose their legs above the knees; this is considered indecent for women but not for men.

Try to remember the Sherpa word for thank you, which is *tuche*; Nepali is *dahnyibaht*.

Staying Healthy

Being fit and healthy when you arrive and staying that way during your stay need not be a problem if the following simple rules are observed. Avoid drinking unboiled water if at all possible. A water bottle which has been filled with treated or boiled water is necessary in the lower areas approaching the Park because almost all streams are polluted, no matter how pure they might appear. Water can be purified by adding four drops of iodine to one litre and waiting twenty minutes before drinking. Iodine crystals and solution are available in Kathmandu. Chlorine is not effective against amoebic dysentery cysts.

Obtaining liquid refreshment is not a problem in the Khumbu as there are dozens of chang and teashops along the main trekking routes. Tea is safe to drink but be cautious of the chang! It is more alcoholic than it tastes and as it is made with unboiled water it can be a source of intestinal trouble.

Try and keep your hands as clean as possible, particularly before eating.

Do not try and force your walking pace to keep up with the group or a friend. Walk at your own pace, the one that feels comfortable to you. Above all take care of your feet; you won't be able to change them for another pair and they need to be happy for the whole trip. If your footwear is chafing, attend to the sore places before blisters develop as a broken blister can turn into a nasty, painful sore.

Do not try to go too high, too soon, or altitude sickness will end your trek before you reach your goal.

This porter's feet may be tough from never wearing shoes, but visitors need to ensure that theirs are well cared for during a trek.

At high altitudes the human body needs time to adjust to the lack of oxygen in the air. When ascending it is important that sufficient time is allowed for this acclimatisation to take place, or altitude sickness can have extremely serious effects. Experienced trekkers take this into account when planning a trip.

Acute Mountain Sickness (AMS)

Altitude sickness can be a dangerous health hazard in the Himalaya. In past years many trekkers have died or become seriously ill, lacking an awareness of the problems of altitude. A basic knowledge of the problem can help to avoid unnecessary deaths or complicated rescue attempts.

The Himalaya are the highest mountains in the world, beginning where most other mountains leave off. Even experienced mountaineers tend to forget this. Previous mountaineering experience may increase fitness and trekking ability, but it does not usually prepare a person for the problems of staying at high altitudes. As a person ascends, his body begins making elaborate adjustments to adapt to the thinner air; but these changes take time. This period of adjustment is called acclimatisation. Any planned trek in Sagarmatha National Park must allow for acclimatisation before the higher altitudes are attempted.

A schedule of ascent in this region, which will allow the average trekker to ascend safely, has been developed by the Himalayan Rescue Association (H.R.A.) who have researched the problem. For some, though, it will still be too fast. Do not plan to ascend faster than this rate. Symptoms of Acute Mountain Sickness can appear at any time above 2500 metres, and must be looked for. Remember, if a person is not doing well at altitude, to assume that it is altitude sickness until proved otherwise. The actual symptoms can be subtle and variable.

The specific symptoms to look for include: a headache that persists through the day, loss of appetite, nausea, vomiting, swelling of the hands and face, weakness, and (very serious), a loss of co-ordination. These are all symptoms of High Altitude Cerebral Oedema (waterlogged brain). Unusual breathlessness at rest, rapid pulse, cough and chest pains are symptoms of High Altitude Pulmonary Oedema (waterlogged lungs). Both are Acute Mountain Sickness. Any or all of these symptoms can occur separately or together.

Minor symptoms can be treated by resting at the same altitude for an extra day. If the symptoms are becoming progressively worse or the trekker is significantly affected by them and unable to eat or walk without assistance, he or she should descend immediately, either day or night. The earlier a person descends, the less descent is necessary for marked improvement. Often a 300 to 600 metre descent will improve the patient dramatically. The importance of having a person descend under his own power while still capable of doing so can not be overstressed. Try not to let your ego or ambitions cloud your judgement in relation to making an appropriate early descent. If you have only a limited time in the area you must accept the fact that you are not able to go very high. A person with mountain sickness may not be capable of making correct decisions, so a responsible trek leader may have to insist that they descend even against their will.

Group treks arranged through trekking agencies offer the advantage of an experienced guide and Sherpa support in emergencies. A relative disadvantage is that members are tied to fixed schedules and all members may not acclimatise at the same rate. Each trekking group should have provision to allow slower acclimatisers to remain behind or descend as necessary, apart from the main group.

Solo trekkers can usually have a more flexible schedule, but the disadvantage is that there will be little support in an emergency. Therefore the solo trekker should be alert for symptoms and descend when appropriate. If necessary, porters can be hired at any village to assist in descending, and there are also a few yaks available which can carry people.

The option of trekking with a group or going it alone should be fully considered before coming to the Park. Both ways have advantages and disadvantages, but for the solo trekker, without the support of a trekking organisation, problems of altitude sickness can be more serious.

Recommended Itinerary of Ascent

1st night: between Lukla and Jorsalle 2nd night: Namche Bazar
3rd night: Namche Bazar 4th night: Tengboche
5th night: Pheriche 6th night: Pheriche
7th night: Lobuche 8th night: Lobuche, Gorak Shep
or Base Camp.

This schedule can be varied to include sleeping at other places, as long as two nights are spent at the same altitude twice between Lukla and Lobuche. The rest days can be spent hiking to higher altitudes and returning to sleep, or just resting at the same height.

No medicine can be recommended to allow a more rapid ascent, but Diamox (acitazolumide) is often helpful when minor symptoms occur, or for related sleep problems.

174

Additional Points

Dehydration is a constant threat at altitude due to breathing heavily in the cold dry air. Thirst is not a reliable indicator of body water needs, so it is wise to make an attempt to drink as much as possible during the day, at least three to four litres.

Oral contraceptives should not be taken at altitude because of potential blood clotting problems.

Children, and people under 21, are many times more susceptible to A.M.S. and should be watched closely.

The majority of people complete their treks without serious problems. Don't let unnecessary fear cloud your enjoyment, but be alert for the symptoms of A.M.S. and be mentally prepared to descend if necessary. If you descend with early symptoms, re-ascent is possible after all the symptoms have gone. Those people who descend with serious symptoms, however, such as loss of co-ordination or severe breathlessness, should not plan to re-ascend on the same trek.

Rescue

The Himalayan Rescue Association usually maintains a trekkers' Aid Post at Pheriche, staffed by a physician and trained Sherpa assistants, during the two trekking seasons. Their job is to advise people about the problems of altitude, treat them when necessary, and help arrange rescues when appropriate. If a person is having problems above Pheriche, do not send for the doctor or a helicopter and then await rescue — carry or assist the person down. Always accompany a person with severe symptoms. The descent will usually bring a marked improvement and the Pheriche doctor can then offer aid as necessary. Even if given treatment by a doctor, a patient will still have to go down because there is no substitute for descent.

There is a hospital at Khunde, staffed by a doctor and Sherpa assistants, where trekkers can receive help.

It is a mistake to rely on helicopter evacuation. Although life-saving at times, radio communications are difficult, helicopters are not always available and can take up to 24 hours or more to arrive. Even if one were available it would not come unless some guarantee of payment is made in Kathmandu. This can be organised by a good trekking agency for its clients, but is almost impossible for individual trekkers. Plan on descending by foot if at all possible. There is usually no provision for bodies to be flown out of the mountains, and cremation is best arranged on site.

Yesterday, Today, Tomorrow

Toward a Better Life

The first successful ascent of Sagarmatha by Sir Edmund Hillary and Tenzing Norgay Sherpa had far reaching effects for the Sherpas. Hillary greatly admired their cheerfulness, gentle natures and bodily strength, and knew that without their help mountaineering expeditions would struggle to reach their objectives.

Sir Edmund was keen to assist the Sherpas to better their families' lives, but knew that aid in the form of cash donations would do little to help. Their needs were for education, medical services and practical things such as improved bridges and water supplies. Since 1953 Sir Edmund has worked at raising money for the various projects and facilities requested by the Sherpas, with the Himalayan Trust being formed to administer the funds. A primary policy of the Trust was never to instigate projects but to respond to requests from the Sherpa communities. A condition of their assistance has always been the involvement of the local community, contributing in the form of physical labour and some materials.

In 1961, at the conclusion of the Himalayan Scientific and Mountaineering Expedition 1960-61, Hillary and his team, with the co-operation of His Majesty's Government of Nepal, built the first school at Khumbjung. This initial building was of prefabricated aluminium construction and is still in use. After Khumbjung School was built there were requests from many other villages, wanting schools for their children. When Hillary returned to Khumbu in 1963 he brought materials for more projects. Again His Majesty's Government of Nepal gave its endorsement and co-operation. Pipes were laid to improve the water supplies to Khunde and Khumbjung villages, and schools were built at Pangboche and Thami. During this expedition, when an epidemic of smallpox broke out, the team was able to immunise most of the people of Khumbu and areas to the south in the Dudh Kosi valley. Arising from this incident, the first medical clinic for the Sherpas was started in a tent. It was soon shifted to a room in Khumbjung Gompa and operated for the six months that the expedition was in the area. A more permanent medical facility became a reality when Khunde Hospital was opened on December 18th 1966. The original hospital has been enlarged and today caters for all Sherpas who require medical attention, giving advice and aid to trekkers when necessary. The Khunde doctors also hold regular clinics at other villages in and beyond the Park, providing immunisation, family planning and general health care.

With more Sherpa parents wanting education for their children, the original school at Khumbjung was added to in 1968 and now has three classrooms, and carpentry and handcraft rooms. In 1979 a small hostel was built to provide older, higher-level pupils, from more distant villages such as Pangboche and Thami, with accommodation during the week.

In addition to building schools and water supplies, in 1964 the Himalayan Trust built a substantial bridge across the Dudh Kosi, near Jorsalle, and another over the Bhote Kosi. Devastating glacial outburst floods have since destroyed both these bridges; the one near Jorsalle in 1977 and the other over the Bhote Kosi in 1986.

Lukla airstrip was also built in 1964, allowing much easier access to the Khumbu region. As a consequence tourism boomed. The original airstrip was lengthened in 1966 and later widened at the top to provide more turning room for planes.

178

Opportunities for education are welcomed and sought after, and school is a regular part of most Sherpa children's day. Khumbjung School, built by Sir Edmund Hillary and the Himalayan Trust in 1961, has provided many children with a sound basis for further education.

Medical care and health education for individuals and whole communities are provided by the Himalayan Trust Hospital at Khunde. This community facility was opened in 1966 and is staffed by trained doctors from New Zealand and Canada, and local assistants and trainees.

Other agencies have also co-operated with His Majesty's Government in providing projects in the Khumbu region. The New Zealand Government's involvement began in 1974 when a joint task force of officials from New Zealand and Nepal made an assessment of the possibilities for development of the national park, and recommended a programme for bilateral co-operation. Over the following six years New Zealand national park rangers and foresters lived in Khumbu, working with Nepalese to set up the Park and reafforestation programme. The park building programme included overnight trekking lodges, staff quarters and a Visitor Centre. A Park Management Plan was drawn up and many of the recommendations are being implemented. These projects all involved locally recruited park staff, some of whom were selected for further management training in New Zealand.

The trekkers' lodges at Tengboche, Pheriche and Lobuche were designed to provide a good standard of overnight accommodation and were intended also as a demonstration of how alternative fuels could be used for cooking and heating. The programme also built the suspension bridge spanning the narrow gorge between Tengboche and Pangboche, improving access to the upper areas of the Park.

Sir Edmund Hillary and a team of willing local helpers repair a bridge over the Bhote Kosi River, below Namche Bazar. Revered by the Sherpas because of the assistance he has provided through the Himalayan Trust, this bridge is a typical example of the practical help given.

2

The traditional cantilevered bridge such as this (1) usually succumbed to monsoon floods each summer, isolating villages of Khumbu from each other and the rest of Nepal. This one at Phunki Tenga has now been replaced by a suspension bridge (2) built with assistance of American Peace Corps volunteers.

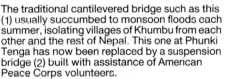

1

The substantial bridge across the Dudh Kosi at Phunji Tenga was built by American Peace Corps volunteers in 1982.

Assistance towards the religious and cultural aspects of the Sherpas' lives has not been overlooked either. Khumbjung Gompa was reroofed in 1966 by the Himalayan Trust and His Majesty's Government and in 1970 and 1984 they carried out extensive structural repairs to Thami Gompa. Funds for the upkeep of religious and cultural sites are now available through UNESCO because the Park is a World Heritage Site.

In addition to the Australian-financed hydro-electric scheme on the Dhute Kosi River, there are two mini-hydro plants. Jointly financed by His Majesty's Government and UNESCO World Heritage Committee, the one at Namche generates enough electricity for lighting the village and some cooking. The other mini-hydro plant, built in the Phunki Drangka in 1988 to supply Tengboche with electricity, was funded jointly by UNESCO, His Majesty's Government, the Himalayan Foundation and the King Mahendra Trust for Nature Conservation.

181

The Forests — A Vanishing Resource

"The single most important problem is the condition of the Khumbu Forests". —
Polly Cooper, student of Environmental Planning, in paper 'Tourism
Development in Nepal', case study, July 1974.

Ten years later the continued depletion of these forests is still the single
major problem.

Traditionally the forests were used by the Sherpas for fuel wood, building
and craft material, as animal grazing areas, and the leaf litter from them for
compost. Because of the influence of the old Sherpa law, only dead wood
was collected for fuel. It is lighter to carry and easier to burn. Until the mid
1950's strict laws on forest conservation were enforced by the villagers
themselves, with the election of Forest Guardians. These men had the right
to regulate the areas of forest which fuel wood or timber could or could not
be taken from. Their success at forest conservation was notable.

With the nationalisation of forests and grazing lands in 1957, and a new
political system introduced in 1963, control was placed in the hands of the
central government system. The influence of the Forest Guardians was
minimised and the traditional restraints on forest utilisation weakened, but
not effectively replaced by new controls. With the closure of the Tibetan
border in 1959 the Sherpas also lost their trading links and associated
incomes. The trading was replaced by servicing the growing number of
expeditions and trekkers, all of whom wanted firewood and other services
such as food supplies and porters etc. Firewood then became a cash crop for
which tourists and expeditions were prepared to pay large sums of money.
Green wood was then cut because it weighed more.

Firewood consumption by the large expeditions was high. It has been
estimated that each expedition used four 30 kilogram loads per day (120
kilograms) and as each expedition stayed in the Park for approximately two
months it used about 240 loads, or 7200 kilograms of firewood. In 1979 there
were four expeditions in the Park, each staying between two and three
months. Their firewood consumption has been estimated at about 960
loads, or 28,000 kilograms.

Previously the Sherpas had survived by selling their surplus potatoes,
trading with Tibet, and selling dairy products, but they now had a quicker
and easier way to earn money. Even though some Sherpas could see future
problems they did nothing to stop the practice of selling firewood. If they
stopped selling it someone else would take the advantage and make money
instead. They all needed incomes.

Because of the hotel trade and firewood sales, the people living along the
main trekking routes have been the ones who have profited most from
tourism. With more regular incomes they have been able to cope with the
higher prices for basic goods which tourism has brought. The villagers
living away from the main trekking routes have consequently suffered as
this inflation has also affected them.

For the Sherpas the scarcity of wood is becoming a problem. It now takes
as long to walk to an area where they can find wood as it does to make up a
load. For Khumbjung people this is two hours of walking each way, and
another two hours of searching before they have enough wood for one
load. The wealthier households can afford to keep servants solely to collect

firewood, but for poorer people it is becoming increasingly difficult. They must collect wood themselves, and the time spent collecting wood can not be used to earn money from other occupations.

Tourism has had another equally important impact. With the increased wealth that it brought, larger houses and hotels were built, using more wood in construction, and for cooking and heating. Larger herds of yaks, or even non-traditional animals such as goats were kept and the increased animal numbers put more pressure on an already overgrazed land and fragile environment.

The leaf litter collected from the forest is very important to the Sherpas as a source of fertiliser. It is laid down on the ground floors of their houses, and also in lavatories.

Once a much too familiar sight, yaks carry loads of firewood up the Khumbu Glacier to the Base Camp site. Before regulations were implemented, banning its use by visitors, firewood was an earner of cash and vast quantities were consumed by large international expeditions and trekking groups.

Almost hidden by the huge basket she carries, a young Sherpani brings a load of leaf litter from the forest, to be used in cattle byres. Mixed with manure it makes essential fertilizer for crops. Unfortunately, removal of this litter from the forest floor adversely affects regeneration of the trees by removing seed, and nutrients that would normally be recycled.

In spring the old leaves and manure are removed and dug into the fields before the crops are planted. As this is the only fertiliser available it is essential for maintaining crop productivity, and hence the peoples' welfare. Unfortunately, removal of forest litter affects the regeneration of young seedlings under the forest canopy.

An indication of the size to which trees once grew can be gained from the width of floor planks in older houses. They measure well over half a metre. It would be difficult now to find a tree large enough to provide timber this size. The name Namche means *'shaded by forest'* but although older Sherpas can remember trees on the slopes above the village, there are none there today. Protected trees in the vicinity of *gompas* are examples of how the forests must have once looked.

The juniper tree still has traditional uses, with its green foliage being burnt on household altars for religious purposes. When a son is born a juniper spar is erected outside the house. This ceremony is called *gotar*, and the tree for it must be tall enough for its top to reach the roof. Religion also requires that the trunk of a fir tree be erected outside the small chapel of each house, with a cloth attached to it, printed with the Buddhist moral code. This is called *chotar*. Unfortunately it is now difficult to find trees tall enough for *gotar* and *chotar*.

Reafforestation

As well as the critical shortage of firewood which has developed with the depletion of the forests, there is also an altered landscape and an increasing ecological imbalance. In an effort to improve the situation, and as part of the New Zealand contribution toward the National Park, a reafforestation programme was commenced. By replanting areas which have become denuded it is hoped that some forests will become re-established, using faster growing species such as the Blue Pine which is an aggressive coloniser. With careful management the forests could have returned naturally in time if left undisturbed, however it is now no longer possible for this to happen. The only alternative is the artificial establishment of forest which, with correct management, will go a long way to restoring the Park to its former state.

The first tree nursery was started in 1978 just below Namche Bazar, beside the main trail leading into the village. It was from here that the initial pine, fir and rhododendron seedlings, were planted out. A second nursery was developed near Teshinga, just below the main trail to Tengboche, and others have also been established at Jorsalle, Phortse and Phurte (near Thamo).

The seedlings need two years in the nursery before being planted out. After that they still need protection from trampling by grazing animals if they are to survive, so planted areas are encircled with fences or stone walls. The walls are thick enough to withstand the advances of large yaks which find the lush growth within very tempting, in comparison to the sparse ground cover elsewhere.

The nurseries are capable of producing 100,000 seedlings each year, and provide alternative employment for local people. Fresh seeds are collected from the mature forests annually. With pine and fir trees this entails picking the ripe cones from the trees, and then extracting and drying the seeds before they are planted in individual pots. The seedlings must then be kept watered and free of weeds until they are large enough to leave the nursery, jobs which are done mainly during late spring and summer when there is little tourist traffic and other employment.

The forest species which are found in the Park grow relatively fast compared to other northern hemisphere conifers, but only slowly above 3500 metres, so it will be some time before results of the work already done are visible. Even the faster growing Blue Pine needs from forty to fifty years to attain a substantial size. In the meantime it is hoped that demands for firewood will decrease as a result of advances in technology with other forms of cooking and heating, and better supplies of alternative fuels.

Employment and practical demonstration are provided by the reafforestation programme. Ripe cones are picked from the Blue Pine and Silver Fir each year. From these the seed is collected and dried before planting in nurseries.

The Future

Sagarmatha is a Park on which the eyes of the world focus. All who visit this magnificent area will be concerned at the critical state of its forests, and many will ask "What is its future"? — a very valid question. The Khumbu region does have a future, and many steps have already been taken to ensure it.

One of the first was the formation of a National Park, giving protection by law, and a status which recognises the uniqueness of the area, setting it above the rest of the land. Recognition as a World Heritage Site adds to its importance. With the establishment of the Park, regulations were brought in, including an important ban on the use of firewood by tourists, who must now be self-sufficient in alternative fuels when they enter the Park. Although Sherpas may collect firewood for their own use, it is illegal for them to sell it to visitors. These are regulations which must be adhered to by both groups otherwise they will do little to ease the situation. As in Nepal's other National Parks, the Royal Nepalese Army was brought in to help enforce the new regulations. Guards stationed at Phunki Tenga, Thami and Namche Bazar make regular patrols into the forests to check for any illegal cutting of green wood or damage to trees, while their other protective role is against poaching of the Musk Deer. A poacher can expect severe penalties if caught.

The reafforestation programme is an ongoing project with the nurseries, replanting and fencing now mostly financed by the Himalayan Trust. It is sometimes argued that there must be exotic tree species which would grow faster than the pine and fir within the Parks high altitudes, solving the firewood problem in a short time. This is possibly correct, however the area is a National Park, its status precluding the establishment of exotic forests within its boundaries. All attempts must be made to keep or return the land to as natural a state as possible. Exotic tree species could overtake the existing natural vegetation, irreversibly altering the present ecosystem.

Further down the Dudh Kosi valley outside the Park boundaries where it is warmer, opportunities exist for producing firewood from exotics. With active management the existing forests at lower altitudes could also provide firewood without their being exploited as they have been in the past.

The eradication of goats from the Park was another, less obvious, step taken to protect the vegetation. Goats were never a traditional animal of the Sherpas, as they are with other ethnic groups in Nepal who use them for meat. As more people from these other groups came to reside in Khumbu, more and more goats were brought into the Park. Goats are very destructive, unlike the traditional cattle, which are selective and do not destroy vegetation when they browse as they are unable to bite the grass off at ground level. Goats are non-selective eaters and will chew plants off to the roots, denuding an area before moving on to another. The Himalayan Trust, with the support of the local people and the Department of National Parks and Wildlife Conservation, purchased all the goats in the Park and had them removed. An agreement was then arranged so that no more goats would be kept.

Some progress has already been made in making stoves which are more economical with fuel and provide more heat than the traditional open fires or ovens. The use of these is increasing, many having attachments which heat water without extra fuel being used. Electric energy is also being produced in very small amounts and there are plans for more hydro-electric schemes, although how appropriate they are in a National Park is an aspect that has been questioned. Electrical appliances are also of questionable value to the Sherpas, at present, as they are generally unavailable in Nepal, and beyond the means of most of its citizens.

Greater use of alternative fuels is not the complete answer. Nepal must import all of its petroleum-based products, so an alternative fuel such as kerosene is an expensive commodity which most people are unable to afford.

Occasionally supplies of kerosene are rationed in Kathmandu and when this happens there is little hope of any reaching remote regions such as the Khumbu. All efforts to use alternative fuels where possible should be made at present, however the next question which arises is "How long will world supplies of oil last"?

The greatest source of energy in Khumbu is the sun, and ways of harnessing its energy are being developed all the time. A few Sherpa houses already have crude solar panels for heating water but it will be some time before advances in solar technology will be available and cheap enough for all to use. Any new technology must be aesthetically acceptable.

Perhaps the greatest hope for the future lies in education. Sherpa children are being taught the principles of forest conservation and most are aware of the present problems. The reafforestation programme has demonstrated that the trees can be returned fairly simply and easily, so it is hoped that the old traditional values will become re-established as the Sherpas see their forests renewed. Older students are being trained at overseas universities, in national parks and forestry management. They will return to Nepal with more knowledge and better equipped to administer their lands.

Hope for Khumbu's forests grows in the tree nurseries such as this one at Teshinga. The reafforestation project has demonstrated that the trees can be returned to the land, and it is hoped that traditional conservation practices will be re-established as forests are renewed.

187

Visitors to Sagarmatha National Park also share the responsibility of keeping it in the best possible condition. This means abiding by the firewood regulations, not littering, and observing local customs and traditions. Already there are changes in the sizes of groups visiting the Park. There are still large expeditions coming to climb the world's highest summits, but the smaller, more self-contained, alpine-style attempts are becoming more popular, minimizing the need for support staff to huddle round a fire while they wait for the climbers to return from higher camps.

Being part of a large self-sufficient trekking group is still a popular way to visit the Park, however many visitors now come by themselves, relying on local food and accommodation. The large trekking groups provide employment for their many cooks and porters, but they also impose a certain strain on the fragile environment by the very fact that more people make a larger impact. Individual trekkers also make their impact and by relying on local food and accommodation do not provide much employment for porters although they do provide incomes for entrepreneurs who have established themselves in the hotel business.

The Sherpas are a very resilient and adaptable people, and will continue as they have over the centuries. They have shown these strengths with their ability to inhabit a harsh land and survive as traders. When that livelihood was denied to them they successfully and rapidly took on the roles that tourism offered. Their lives have already changed in many respects since the first tourists visited Khumbu, and will continue to change. As an adaptable people they will take advantage of all that western civilisation offers. Who can deny them the advantages of progress? They are not museum pieces to be locked away and kept as mementoes of a bygone era. Tourism has brought the Sherpas a new livelihood and in many cases an improved standard of living, but it has also brought them many problems. There are no easy answers to these problems but if all visitors are aware of them, it will at least be a start to their solution.

This child and others like him hold the future of Khumbu in their hands.

Glossary of Sherpa/Tibetan and Nepali words used in the text and miscellaneous words.

mother
ama
nun
arni
father
ava
hidden valley
beyul
ancient Tibetan religion
Bon
followers of Bon religion
Bon-pos
Tibet
Bhot (Nep)
temple courtyard
cham-ra
rice beer
chang
lavatory
chhakhang
sugar and milk tea
chya (Nep)
religious rite
Chirim
temple guardian
chorpen
religious monument
chorten
temple guardian
chorumba
coat
chu-pah
wedding ceremony
dem-chang
deity spirit
dhu
stream
drangka
religious festival
Dumji
village temple or monastery temple
gompa
low lying summer settlement
gunsa
wedding ceremony
gyen-Kutop
a dress
ingi
blacksmith or metal worker
kami (Nep)
entranceway
kani

artist
kappa
house or home
khangba
river or stream
khola (Nep)
river
kosi (Nep)
a pass
la or lhabtsa
priest
lama
household temple
lhang
main hall in temple
lha-khang
spirit medium
lhawa
new year festival
Losar
deity spirit
lhu
religious offering
mani
religious celebration
Mani Rimdu
stuffed pastry
momo
a fruit
naspati (Nep)
guardian
nawa
religous rite
Niugne
religious rite
Osho
village guardian
osho-nawa
district council system
panchayat (Nep)
hand
pang
festival
Phang-ngi
rice spirits
rakshi (Nep)
mountain
ri
potato
rigi
reincarnated priest
Rimpoche
clan
rhu
potato stew
shakpa
ethnic group or male
sherpa

female
sherpani
wood
shing
forest guardian
shingi-nawa
betrothal ceremony
sodene
salted tea
sol-chya
religious merit
sonam
religious monument
stupa (Nep)
semi precious stone
szi
foot
teng
monk
thawa
scroll painting
thang-ka
noodles
thukpa
oven
thap
small
tickpay
lake
tso
roasted barley/wheat/corn flour
tsampa
thank you
touche
no thank you
touche, touche touche
child
anga
religious celebration
Yer-chang
summer settlement
yersa
turquoise
yhew

VEGETATION SPECIES LIST
Not necessarily exhaustive

Forests
Blue Himalayan pine
Pinus wallichiana
the national flower
Rhododendron arboreum
Rhododendron triflorum
Lily of the valley shrub
Pieris formosa
Himalayan hemlock
Tsuga dumosa
Wallich's yew
Taxus wallichiana
Himalayan oak
Quercus semicarpifolia
Small-leaved cotoneaster
Cotoneaster microphyllus
Scaly rhododendron
Rhododendron lepidotum
Himalayan vine
Parthenocissus himalayense
Mountain clematis
Clematis montana
Campbell's maple
Acer campbellii
Himalayan whitebeam
Sorbus cuspidata
Silver fir
Abies spectabilis
Himalayan birch
Betula utilis
Lichen
Usnea
Tree juniper
Juniperus recurva

Alpine Scrub (lower zone)
Alpine cinquefoil
Potentilla arbuscula
Dwarf rhododendron
Rhododendron setosum
Dwarf rhododendron
Rhododendron anthopogon
Dwarf rhododendron
Rhododendron lepidotum
Dwarf juniper
Juniperus indica
Dwarf juniper
Juniperus squamata
Sikkim willow
Salix sikkimensis
Alpine gentian
Gentiana prolata
Cassiope fastigiata

Himalayan edelweiss
Leontopodium stracheyi
Codonopsis thalictrifolia
Meadow-rue
Thalictrum chelidonii
Nepalese lily
Lilium nepalense
Notholirion macrophyllum
Fritillary
Fritillaria cirrhosa
Himalayan primrose
Primula denticulata
Himalayan primrose
Primula atrodentata
Himalayan primrose
Primula woolastonii
Himalayan primrose
Primula sikkimensis
Milk-vetches
Astragalus species

Alpine Scrub (upper zone)
Snow rhododendron
Rhododendron nivale
Himalayan buckthorn
Hippophae thibetana
Alpine shrubby horsetail
Ephedra gerardiana
Black juniper
Juniperus indica
Shrubby cinquefoil
Potentilla arbuscula
Ornate gentian
Gentiana ornata
Przwalski's mountain gentian
Gentiana algida var przwalskii
Edelweiss
Leontopodium jacotianum
Spiny mountain poppy
Meconopsis horridula
Stitchwort
Arenaria polytrichioides
Tanacetum gossypinum

COMMON BUTTERFLIES SPECIES LIST
Common yellow swallowtail
Papilio machaon
Common blue apollo
Parnassius hardwickei
Common red apollo
Parnassius epaphus
Large cabbage white
Pieris brassicae
Indian cabbage white
Pieris canidia

Common brimstone
Gonepteryx rhamni
Dark clouded yellow
Colias fieldii
Pamir clouded yellow
Colias cocandica
Pale hedge blue
Celastrina cardia
Peablue
Lampides boeticus
Green sapphire
Heliophorus androcles
Silver hairstreak
Chrysozephyrus syla
Large silverstripe
Childrena childreni
Queen of Spain fritillary
Issoria issaea
Painted lady
Vanessa cardui
Indian red admiral
Vanessa indica
Indian tortoiseshell
Aglais cashmirensis
Common woodbrown
Zophoessa sidonis
Small woodbrown
Zophoessa nicetella
Barred woodbrown
Zophoessa maitrya
Small silverfork
Zophoessa jalaurida
Small goldenfork
Zophoessa atkinsoni
Brown forester
Lethe serbonis
Small tawny wall
Raphicera moorei
Great satyr
Aulocera padma
Common satyr
Aulocera swaha
Narrow-banded satyr
Aulocera brahminus
Pallid argus
Callerebia scanda
Indian skipper
Spialia galba
Orange and silver
mountain hopper
Carterocephalus avanti

REPTILES SPECIES LIST
Wolf snake
Lycodon aulicus
Striped keelback
Amphiesma stolata
Mountain keelback
Amphiesma platyceps
Boulenger's keelback
Amphiesma parallela
Himalayan keelback
Rhabdophis himalayanus
Mountain pit viper
Trimeresurus monticola
Himalayan pit viper
Agkistrodon himalayanus
Skink
Scincella sikimensis
Garden lizard
Calotes versicolor

AMPHIBIANS SPECIES LIST
Amphibians which occur or probably occur in the Park
Himalayan toad
Bufo himalayanus
Frog
Rana liebigii
Polunin's frog
Rana polunini
Frog
Rana sikimensis
Tree frog
Polypedates maculatus

BIRD SPECIES LIST
Cranes (Gruidae)
Demoiselle crane
Anthropoides virgo

Geese and Ducks (Anatidae)
Bar-headed goose
Anser indicus
Brahminy duck
Tadorna ferruginea
Gadwall
Anas strepera
Common pochard
Aythya ferina
Tufted pochard
Aythya fuligula
Eurasian wigeon
Anas penelope

Dippers (Cindidae)
Brown dipper
Cinclus pallasii

Kites, Hawks, Eagles, Vultures, and Allies (Accipitridae)
Dark kite
Milvus migrans
Golden eagle
Aquila chrysaetos
Steppe eagle
Aquila nipalensis
Himalayan griffon
Gyps himalayensis
Lammergeier
Gypaetus barbatus

Partridges and Pheasants (Phasianidae)
Tibetan snow-cock
Tetraogallus tibetanus
Blood pheasant
Ithaginis cruentus
Impeyan pheasant (the national bird)
Lophophorus impejanus

Gulls (Laridae)
Black-headed gull
Larus ridibundus
Brown-headed gull
Larus brunnicephalus

Pipits and Wagtails (Motacillidae)
Rose-breasted pipit
Anthus roseatus

Finches and Allies (Fringillidae)
Beautiful rose-finch
Carpodacus pulcherrimus
Brandt's mountain finch
Leucosticte brandti
Common rose finch
Carpodacus erythrinus
Red-breasted rose finch
Carpodacus puniceus
Pink-browed rose finch
Carpodacus rhodochrous

Pigeons (Columbidae)
Snow pigeon
Columba leuconota

Owls (Tytonidae and Strigidae)
Tawny wood owl
Strix aluco

Larks (Alaudidae)
Horned lark
Eremophila alpestris

Crows and Allies (Corvidae)
Jungle crow
Corvus macrorhynchos
Raven
Corvus corax
Red-billed chough
Pyrrhocorax pyrrhocorax
Yellow-billed chough
Pyrrhocorax graculus

Minivets and Allies (Campedhagidae)
Long-tailed minivet
Pericrocotus ethologus

Babblers, Laughing Thrushes, and Allies (Timaliidae)
White-browed tit babbler
Alcippe vinipectus
Black-throated thrush
Turdus ruficollus
Parrotbill
Paradoxornis

Warblers (Sylviidae)
Orange-barred leaf warbler
Phylloscopus pulcher

Thrushes, Chats, and Allies (Turdidae)
Orange-flanked bush robin
Erithacus cyanurus
White-browed robin
Erithacus indicus
Grandala
Grandala coelicolor
Plumbeous redstart
Rhyacornis fuliginosus
White-capped river chat
Chaimarrornis leucocephus
White throated redstart
Phoenicurus schisticeps
Chestnut-bellied rock thrush
Monticola rufiventris

Accentors (Prunellidae)
Alpine accentor
Prunella collaris
Robin accentor
Prunella rubeculoides
Rufous-breasted accentor
Prunella strophiata

Titmice (Paridae)
Coal tit
Parus ater
Crested brown tit
Parus dichrous
Sikkim black tit
Parus rubidiventris beavani

Wall creepers (Sittidae)
Northern tree creeper
Certhia familiaris

MAMMALS SPECIES LIST
Mammals which occur or
probably occur in the Park

Insectivora
Short-tailed mole
Talpa micura
Tibetan water shrew
Nectogale elegans
Himalayan water shrew
Chimmarrogale himalayica
Brown-toothed shrew
Soriculus caudatus

Primates
Rhesus monkey
Macaca mulatta
Langur
Presbytis entallus

Lagomorpha
Himalayan mouse-hare
Ochotana royelei
Woolly Himalayan hare
Lepus oiostilus

Rodentia
House rat
Rattus rattoides
House mouse
Mus musculus

Carnivora
Lesser panda
Ailurus fulgens
Himalayan wolf
Canis lupus
Jackal
Canis aureus
Snow leopard
Panthera unica
Himalayan palm civet
Paguma larvata
Himalayn weasel
Mustela sibirica

Yellow-throated marten
Martes flavigula
North Indian marten
Charronia flavigula
Tibetan polecat
Mustela putorius
Alpine vole
Pitymys sikimensis
Himalayan marmot
Marmot babak Himalayana
Himalayan black bear
Selenarctos thibetanus
Mountain fox
Vulpes montana

Artiodactyla
Musk deer
Moschus moschiferus
Himalayan tahr
Hemitragus jemlahicus
Yak
Bos grunniens

Chiroptera
Leaf-nosed bat
Hipposideros armiger
Short-nosed fruit bat
Cyanoptera sphinx

Acknowledgements

Principal Authors: Margaret Jefferies, Margaret Clarbrough
Contributors: Dr. Robert Fleming Jr. (Birds), Tony Schilling (Flora), Colin Smith (Butterflies), Dr. David Schlim (Acute Mountain Sickness)
The authors would like to thank the following people for their useful advice and comments: Ian Whitehouse, Mal Clarbrough (Geology), Peter and Penny Gorman, Lawrie and Kay Halkett (Forestry), Dr. John McKinnon (Himalayan Trust), Janice Sacherer, Lhakpa Norbu Sherpa, Mingma Norbu Sherpa, Pemba Tsering Sherpa (The People). Special thanks also to the staff of Ministry of Foreign Affairs in Wellington and London, Lester Clark of Department of Lands and Survey, and staff of the National Parks and Wildlife Conservation Office, Kathmandu for their assistance.
Project Co-ordinator: Bruce Jefferies
Editorial Advisor: Joan Poulton
Art Direction, Design and Graphics: Leonard Cobb
Typesetting: Linoset Services Ltd
Map: Department of Lands and Survey, Wellington
Photography: Bruce Jefferies, Mike Edginton, Mal Clarbrough, Martin Heine, Mary-Rose Fowlie, Peter Gorman, Brian Hunt.
British Alpine Club, p.138, 140, 145
Royal Geographic Society, p.138, 139
Bruce Coleman Ltd, p.79 (Red panda)
Gerald Cubitt/Bruce Coleman Ltd, p.79 (marmot); Norman Tomalin/Bruce Coleman Ltd, p.79 (Snow leopard)
Joanna van Gruisen/Survival Anglia, p.79 (Himalayan bear)

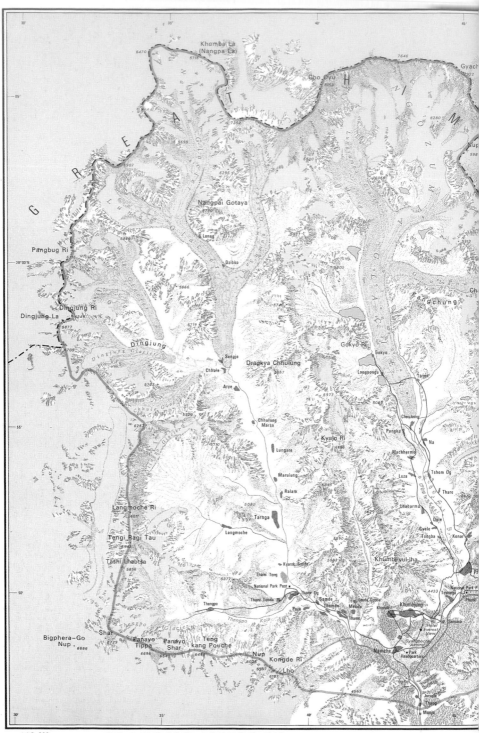

Base information obtained from the Royal Geographical Society map "Mount Everest Region".